D1595104

Making Forest of Bliss

Intention, Circumstance, and Chance in Nonfiction Film

A conversation between

Robert Gardner + Ákos Östör

Publication of this book
has been supported
by a generous grant from
the Rock Foundation,
New York.

© 2001
by the President
and Fellows
of Harvard College

All rights reserved

Voices and
Visions in Film

Series Editor
Bruce Jenkins,
Harvard Film Archive

Designer
Lorraine Ferguson

Film Study Center,
Production and
Technical Assistance
Kristi Barlow
Kyle Gilman
Alex Olch
Jacqueline Soohen

Cover photo
Christopher James

All other images
© Robert Gardner 2001

DVD Producer
DVD Labs
Somerville
Massachusetts

Printing
Eurasia Press
Singapore

Forest of Bliss
is the subject of numerous articles
and reviews available at:
www.filmstudycenter.org/makingforestofbliss

All inquiries regarding the film should be directed to the
Film Study Center
Harvard University
Cambridge, Massachusetts 02138

Library of Congress Cataloging-in-Publication Data

Gardner, Robert, 1925–
    Making Forest of bliss : intention, circumstance, and chance
    in nonfiction film : a conversation between Robert Gardner + Ákos Östör.
        p. cm. — (Voices and visions in film)
    Transcription of a conversation held toward the end of Apr. 1987.
    Includes bibliographical references.
    ISBN 0-674-00787-5
        1. Vârânasi (India) — Social life and customs.
2. Forest of bliss (Motion picture) I. Title: Forest of bliss.
II. Östör, Ákos. III. Harvard Film Archive. IV. Forest of bliss.
V. Title. VI. Series.
DS486.B4 G38 2001
954'.2 — dc21   2001039410

Contents

Foreword

Robert Gardner

TOWARD THE END of April 1987, Ákos Östör and I recorded an informal conversation about my film *Forest of Bliss*. We were prompted by a desire to rescue from fading consciousness our many reflections on an undertaking that ended with the film's completion in 1985. We decided to submit our waning memories of that remarkable episode to an unhurried viewing and reviewing of the film in the hope that we could retrieve the experience of those now distant weeks spent living and working together in Benares. To the extent we have succeeded, those who profess a concern for that imperfectly understood and, critically speaking, neglected enterprise called nonfiction filmmaking may find some modest reward in these pages. Failing that, I have much enjoyed this exploration into various mysteries of the filmmaker's art with an old friend and wise companion.

Reading now what was uttered so long ago, I am struck by how much was left unsaid. For me, every shot in the film launches an exercise in recollection. This might be what this kind of imagery does best, and all that Ákos and I have done is to invite a wider conversation among those who will be seeing the film for the first time.

Forest of Bliss first entered the arena of independent, nonfiction film fifteen years ago, when there was an opportunity to find an audience in both theatrical and nontheatrical distribution. There was also television, of course, which was how most people saw this kind of film. Now everything is changing, and new media—including VHS video, laserdisc, CD–ROM, and DVD—are replacing film as standard modes of presentation.

To produce *Making* Forest of Bliss: *Intention, Circumstance, and Chance in Nonfiction Film,* the transcribed conversation was illustrated with pertinent frames captured from the film by computer. A shot list and bibliography have been added to make possible further inquiry into the union between filmmaking and anthropology. The product is a hard-copy text accompanied by a high-definition rendering of the film on a digital videodisc.

This enterprise was given its initial look by Dana Bonstrom and final shape by Lorraine Ferguson. Nearly everyone in the Film Study Center at Harvard University has participated in some way in its production, and I am grateful to each of them. I give my deepest thanks to an old friend, Stanley Cavell, whose teaching and writing have touched everyone who makes and looks at film.

— Harvard University, 2001

Foreword

Ákos Östör

FOREST OF BLISS was made unusually quickly, in a few months during the cold season of 1984–85. Its roots go back many years to when Robert Gardner and I began a collaborative enterprise at Harvard to produce anthropological films. Between 1982 and 1985 we made three films (two of them with Allen Moore) about sacred ritual in Vishnupur, West Bengal *(Loving Krishna, Sons of Shiva, Serpent Mother)*. Each of our co-productions took a different approach to the combination of film and anthropology. During the months of research preceding and following the filming of *Forest of Bliss* we worked in close association with Dr. Baidyanath Saraswati, R. L. Maurya, and Om Prakash Sharma of the N. K. Bose Memorial Foundation in Benares. The process was long and arduous, but Bob Gardner, mentor in matters cinematic, disciple in matters South Asian, has remained most of all friend and fellow journeyman.

Many years have passed since I sat down with Bob to record this conversation. It was unrehearsed, and I have made minimal changes to the text. It was only after the discussion that I realized the ethnography we routinely allude to might need more detailed commentary. I wrote the missing parts and published them as *"Forest of Bliss:* Film and Anthropology" in the *East-West Film Journal,* vol. 8, no. 2 (July 1994). The essay provides a broad ethnographic context, discussing, among other things, the three main "characters" of the film; the deities, boatmen, sacred sites, animals, and objects used; and—above all—the cremation rites we deal with in rather abbreviated form at the end of the conversation.

I visited Benares many times, both before and after making the film. The production took barely ten weeks—and hard, exhilarating weeks they were! In all, I lived about six or seven months in Benares then, carrying out research for the film with support from the Smithsonian Institution. It was a place and time I shall never forget: hardly a day passes that I do not return to Benares, even if fleetingly, to reflect on death, passing, and liberation.

— **Wesleyan University, 2001**

Introduction
Stanley Cavell

IT WAS CLEAR enough from the first screening of *Forest of Bliss* that the virtual absence of (Western) words from its sound track was meant to intensify the experience of its images together with its remaining sounds, including those of an incomprehensible tongue, as well, I suppose, as to declare by so pervasively fateful an artistic choice precisely that such a film (Gardner characteristically calls his works the results of nonfiction filmmaking), whose worth is tied to how thoroughly the filmmaker has put himself into the hands of chance, is at the same time—which is to say at all its moments—pervaded with choice. But there was, even at first, a sense of something more at stake. The absence of words magnified my own silence, or say, it called my silence into question.

What is this behavior often called viewing a film? Robert Gardner and Ákos Östör most frequently call those whom they imagine assembled for the film they are revisiting its audience. Do they suggest thereby that we are to listen to these images? If you wish to explain our sitting in silence before a film by saying that it is a matter of courtesy or of practicality (but not all audiences behave, or behaved, so), then how will you explain the breaking of silence afterward—I mean, explain either the characteristic awkwardness in being obliged to say something or other after long silence together or else the reluctance to say anything, that is, to break the spell? What has happened to us? And when do we expect to answer, or start answering, such a question? Who is in a position to receive an answer? Each of the arts will negotiate these crossroads in its own ways. (I will continue to speak as though the audience of film is essentially plural—not, however, as with theater, necessarily more than two at a time.)

For Gardner and Östör there came a time for taking up such questions systematically (or consecutively), for encouraging conversation about *Forest of Bliss* by breaking their own silence about it from within their privileged positions as companions in its origins. I know of no other exchange about a single film quite like this, one in which those most responsible for its inception and realization recall and reflect upon their experiences, past and present, in the face of a full run-through of the film. But while they take the time they need, there is a current of urgency throughout their exchange which I attribute to an idea that they are attempting to prepare the, let's call it, afterlife of the film: to do for it something of what Walter Benjamin claims that translation does for a literary work. I am going on my own experience here of finding a translation of a book of mine to be gratifying in the difficulties it poses—its resistances registering the strength of its language—but reassuring in the evidence it presents that the ability to survive translation is a vital sign that its future life does not depend upon me, is free of me. Of course, their exchange is not meant as a substitute for the film (neither are all translations meant as substitutes), but there is throughout a recurrence to the question of whether the audience will understand a gesture of the film (a cut, a framing, the prolongation of a shot) and whether what the two of them are saying now about a gesture is too private or too crude to be helpful. In part they are concerned that the audience will be unable to read a juxtaposition (of a wild dog and the far shore, of a marigold and a cow and a corpse) as something intended—not so much concerned that the audience will impose a false interpretation on a juxtaposition as that they will fail to understand that there is a mind in view, capable of intention (however restricted in power) and choice (perhaps misguided), and subject to a particular temperament (oddly unlike one's own). In part they are concerned to demonstrate that such things can be talked about with consecutiveness and, so to speak, mutual enlightenment. You can say that the establishment of film studies over the past three decades ought to have provided this demonstration; or you can say that there is a contribution to such studies that filmmakers are in the best position to make.

It may be, however, that *Forest of Bliss* explores a power of film that itself makes intelligence faint: namely, that the very beauty of its images can make one dumb about them, can draw one away from asking what they ask of one—from, as I put it a moment ago, listening to them. (But, of course, without the capacity to be struck dumb, anything one goes on to say will stay at the level of hearsay.) This power of beauty seems not unlike the power Plato credited Socrates with bringing to philosophy, the power to make its presence felt by numbing its recipient, stopping thought, showing philosophy to begin by showing you that you are unprepared for it. One of Gardner's vignettes of his work, not uncharacteristically, reads like a parable (say, a philosophical story) of what he asks of his audience: "I remember as I was following him up the . . . steps above the river, that the sun had come up high enough to feel pretty warm, . . . and that a substantial part of my remaining energy and vigilance had to go into avoiding little mounds of human excrement deposited on these steps earlier in the morning. I was thinking, 'My God, this really is pretty hard on one's sensibilities this early in the morning.' You not only have to think about trying to make a beautiful film but to wonder when some human waste is going to be squeezed up between your toes as you take your next step" (p.41). Beyond being asked to think (about beauty) and to wonder (about excre-ment) without letting the one deny the presence of the other in an imperfect world (I am remembering Gardner's saluting of his old mentor, Luis Buñuel, by recalling that thoughtful

filmmaker's civilized dismissal of Leibniz: "This is not the best of all possible worlds"),
we are asked to take into account that this memory is staged on a flight of steps, under a rising
sun, above the river (all objects whose significance has already been increasing in the film);
and we will eventually be asked to weigh this memory of a net of incessant demands upon the
filmmaker against his particular reaction to this man suddenly banging his head hard against
a stone floor.

It is presumably this interaction of the general and the particular that more than once
gives rise in the conversation provoked by *Forest of Bliss* to the sense of the universal echoes
of the Indian individuality of these events in Benares, derivatives of the fact that all cultures
have, or will be marked by not having, ways to bury and pray and play and fight and owe and
pay and give and obey and forbid and court and copulate and recognize children woven
into their ways of exchanging words. I think I know what it means to say that all cultures have
a religious dimension (say, practices that are uncriticizable by them), but I am not sure that I
know as well what it would mean to say that all have a philosophical dimension (perhaps
a practice of criticizing their practices). So I am interested that when Gardner remarks to Östör
that nearly all the images they have seen store away a fair amount of anthropology, and
Östör replies by adding that, for those who need it, there is also philosophy embedded in the
anthropology, Gardner emphasizes the seriousness of this possibility not, as is characteristic of
his responses, by expanding upon the idea, or turning it in another direction, but by, it seems
to me, shying away from it, studiously shifting the subject onto unargumentative ground:
"Anyway, we are getting closer to Manikarnika" (p.81).

Since I am one who needs philosophy, I would not be content to leave this conversation
without making explicit my sense that philosophy has been repeatedly invited, if not invoked,
throughout these reflections on this reflective film.

Östör at one point seeks to defend his and Gardner's way of understanding another—
another human in another culture—by perceiving how, unlike ants in anthills (p.56),
humans are, as Emerson puts the matter, victims of meaning: fated to think, to regard, and to
bear the regard of others. When Gardner speaks of "people making meaning whenever they
are doing something, even when they are chopping bamboo [to make ladders that are litters],"
Östör mocks the "empiricists' way of deflating such statements" by noting that they will
say, "'Well, he was really only thinking about his breakfast.'" And when he adds that this "may
be true of that particular moment" Gardner satisfyingly responds, "Or even that particular
man" (pp.56–57). Haven't we known deflators of intention forever, people who, discovering that
intention isn't everything wish to make it nothing? A work of philosophy I hope every
anthropologist would ponder (apart from Wittgenstein's *Philosophical Investigations,* whose

stock-in-trade is imagining counter cultures, or counter minds) is J. L. Austin's *How To Do Things With Words:* his discovery of performative speech, which he takes, I think rightly, as the nemesis of those who seek to dissociate themselves from the meaning, or the giving, of their words and deeds by roughly the equivalent of saying they were thinking of their breakfast.

Contrariwise, philosophers would do well to ponder further Gardner's report of his reaction when the man, mentioned earlier, whose journey up a flight of stairs he had carefully followed, ends this sequence of attention, in an access of faith and desire, by banging his head quite hard on the stone floor (pp.52–53). Gardner says he was unprepared for the gesture, and adds: "I was impressed." He knows his reaction to this surprise is significant and stops over it to say that he included the gesture in his film even though it risks being "seen as bizarre"—risks, that is, seeming therefore dismissable rather than, as Gardner finds, particularly revealing. (Gardner here links his perception of the bizarre with "the surrealist realm," thus indicating a relation of his kind of nonfiction filmmaking with a line of fiction films, or poetry.) What is philosophically at stake here, for me, is the idea of the role of impressions, or the impressive, in revealing the world and others in it. The empiricists, from Locke and Hume to Quine, take "impressions" as the basis of our knowledge of our ideas of things and others, which goes with a very particular picture of human experience, one in which the senses link up with the world and others at individual points (Quine calls them "checkpoints"). A counter empiricist such as Emerson (but here he is at one with John Dewey and William James) in effect charges empiricists with not being sufficiently empirical about experience, that is, with confining themselves to a poor sense of experience: one not a function of the variousness of what matters to us, interests us; what counts more for us than something else; what, in a word, impresses us. Wittgenstein in effect associates, without dismissing, the impressive with the bizarre (even, in a sense, with the surrealist) by repeatedly asking us, who are attempting to arrive at philosophical understanding with him, not to accept what we say or do as familiar but as strange, acknowledging our strangeness to ourselves.

It is in this connection that I report an association of mine, even of work of mine, with one of the most remarkable claims Gardner makes for an image he has captured for his film: that of a boy with a kite. "[It] is part of the key notion I wanted to plant in people's minds: that the film starts with the sun rising, . . . being pulled up by that boy who's flying a kite" (p. 39). I associate the slightly mad idea of causing the sun to rise with the passage early in *Walden* in which Thoreau avers that while he never, among his self-appointed tasks at Walden, "assisted the sun materially in his rising," it was nevertheless "of the last importance only to be present at it." It is a characteristically Thoreauvian gag to bring an old-fashioned aspect of a word like *assist* into play, meaning to make oneself present at a social event. The implied claim is that

Thoreau's observance—that is to say, his writing—can make sunrise a communal event even after religion has forgotten how. Long after I knew this about Thoreau's epic testament, derived from his woodland lake, I learned that Heidegger, in his philosophical meditation on Hölderlin's *Ister Hymn* ("Ister" being an early name for a portion of the Danube), reads the poet's line "Now come, fire," said in the presence of the river, as calling up the sun (because being called by its imminent rise). I associate further Thoreau's desire, and resolve, to "anticipate, not the sunrise and dawn merely, but if possible Nature herself!" with Gardner's prophecy concerning his kind of filmmaking: "That there are people who anticipate and others who don't is pretty easy to tell just by looking at a reasonably wide sample of nonfiction films. . . . Not being able to anticipate puts the actuality [i.e., nonfiction] filmmaker at a terrible disadvantage because there is no way to keep that critical, anticipatory instant ahead of what's happening without such an ability" (p. 37).

I put this conjunction of conjurings of the sun together with a passage of the text I prepared for the premiere of *Forest of Bliss* at Harvard's Carpenter Center in 1985, in which I identify various of the motifs of the film—a scavenging dog, a boat gliding, transfiguring fire, as well as the boy flying his kite—as figures for the work of Gardner's camera. Evidently, we must consider that Gardner's camera gives us to understand that it undertakes not to await the sun but to anticipate it by drawing it up.

Not in every mood is one apt to accept such a formulation. But granted the formulation, it seems to me to adumbrate—or say, allegorize—an ambition of nonfiction filmmaking that the beauty and rigor of Gardner's film proves. Does this not provoke us to ask how, in contrast, fiction filmmaking adumbrates and proves its essential ambitions? Would we willingly do without either, and hence without the interplay, of these two branches of the newest of the great arts?

— Harvard University, 2001

Making **Forest of Bliss**

Intention, Circumstance, and Chance
in Nonfiction Film

A conversation between
Robert Gardner + Ákos Östör

FIG. I

<u>RG</u> The film begins with a long fade-in from black leader to a dog trotting along what I call the "far shore" [FIG. I]. This is the first shot of the film. There is an enormous amount to be said about something as singularly important as the first shot of a film, but I should begin by saying something about the idea of the "far shore." It refers to the other, eastern bank of the Ganges. Before I had even arrived in Benares to begin shooting the film, I thought this shore had a special meaning. I sensed a quite forbidding mystery about it. It was a shore as much in the metaphorical sense as any other, something that all of us must finally reach.

It was also a place where the inhabitants of Benares went occasionally for recreation but which, for the most part, they avoided, believing that anyone who died there might be reborn a donkey.

When I began editing the film in April 1985, I put to one side shots that I felt belonged to the domain of the far shore. Most of these shots either were made on that shore or were views of it, usually from the city. A few of them were neither but, nevertheless, seemed to contribute to the notion of being on the "other side"—in the world of death as against the world of life. The opening sequence is consistent in that it all happens on the far shore, from which the first eleven shots were made.

<u>AÖ</u> What is fascinating and will come up throughout our discussion is the difference between the experience of being there— of what was in your mind then, what was in my mind, of what was there in Benares—and how it all came together in the film. This, to me, is a constant source of wonder, even magic, because, obviously, everyone who was there had some image of what was going on and what would or should be in the film. I didn't feel at the time that the other shore had this connotation for you. In fact, you know, the significance of the farther shore for me was one of peace and, in a sense, of relief to be away from the confusion. I always looked forward to going there.

<u>RG</u> **Because of its this-worldly, not its other-worldly possibilities?**

<u>AÖ</u> Yes, and it always was very much a visual experience for me. I had no idea what the film would look like, because that was your responsibility. My responsibility was to apprehend Benares as

an anthropologist would, to interpret visually and otherwise.
I had an idea of what the film might look like, but that had more
to do with what the elements might be that went into it. How
it would come out was an entirely different matter. The "other
shore" question, for me, was tied up with the activities and
animals on that shore. The dogs always had a specifically Benares,
and a generally Indian, civilization significance. It was only
later, when I saw the first assembly of the film, that I realized you
also had a Greek mythological context for these motifs, too.
And again, this is another, for me, amazing matter: that the film
and the image can contain both these connectable references as
well as a whole lot of other things other people bring to the film.

RG   Yes, having been to Benares four or five times before 1984,
I left each time with a better idea of what the place meant
to me and what the place could look like, if I ever made a film
there. I was filling my head with notions about Benares, and one
very distinct and rather compelling feeling was that this place
had a living and a dead side to its river. Then I thought more and
more about it and dragged in, as you mentioned, Greek
sources and ideas. I remember spending some time in the library
looking into Greek mythology and reading again about the
river Styx and about Cerberus and other familiar figures in that
landscape and saying, my God, you know, as I remember
Benares, there really is some reason for seeing a parallel here
between a Greek and a Hindu or Asian idea. I'm not so sure
about all that, but there are these interesting convergences. What
it did for me was to begin to organize the place. I think I was
lucky to have had this idea before getting to Benares, because
this city must be one of the world's most chaotic.
      Returning to the film, I should say that this opening series
of eleven shots, the prologue, is hopefully telling people, perhaps
without them really knowing it is happening, that they are
on the undesirable side of an important river. They are in a place
of death rather than a place of life. One is
looking at Benares across a great river
that is both very real and richly mythical.
Then there is this ambiguity of seeing
something very vital, and that is this dog
that trots along the river bank. This dog is
really full of life.
      The next shot is of a huge ship looming
like some spectral galleon that drifts
across from left to right [FIG. 2]. It's important to see that the movement is from left to

FIG. 2

FIG. 3

right. It's also down river. The boat is going with the current and is just barely seen through an enormously mysterious mist. The next shot is a bird of prey [FIG. 3]. I don't know whether it's a kite or some other kind of hawk. In any case, it is certainly a bird of prey. It is placed here quite intentionally to resonate with other parts of the film where various things appear in the sky, like the boys' paper kites. We're also seeing another element dealing with death.

Then there is that mist, which was such an incredible gift the morning we all went down to look at Manikarnika from the eastern shore. I don't think I had ever seen mist lying so low and so thick on the river. It seemed very urgent, even auspicious, to start shooting this wonderfully mysterious scene. There are times when you know with certainty that what you are looking at you may never see again. The kind of film I wanted to make was going to be influenced by all kinds of contingencies and happenstance, and this misty morning was important in that it came out of the pure accident of weather, which is itself an artifact of the season I happened to be there. Usually people think of Benares as a place of clear skies and great clarity. Well, here is something totally different. You can't even discern the existence of this incredible city because the mist is so thick. For me that was terribly important because it made a mystery. One is forced to wonder what this thing is that's gliding through the mist and what it is that's beyond this mist. What is the mist concealing? All of this was a way to establish a mood more than anything else.

AÖ   Just from the remarks I remember you making, some of these things were important while we were filming. For example, at some point you said that the finished film would perhaps show a few indications of fire very early on, or some visual reference to the sacred fire, leaving a puzzle as to what it might be and yet knowing that it would be cleared up later. So, looking back on it, while much of the finished film was already there in the way you shot it, the way it would add up wasn't entirely clear at the time. It is clearer with hindsight how everything came together in the film.

RG   Yes, I guess we're all in some ways directed by our own obscure inner thinking, our not too accessible thinking about

FIG. 4

FIG. 5

FIG. 6

these things, and that is what is really informing both our eyes and cameras. I probably couldn't have said at all coherently what the film was going to be like, but I always knew certain things had to be shot or I wouldn't be faithful to what I came to feel was something like a vision. Some things simply had to become images. The other thing that might be mentioned here as we try to get more deeply into the film is that the sounds are terribly important. The sound I wanted to predominate here, and I think it does, is the sound of the creaking oarlocks. This sound, in these early passages of the film, is almost the only clear indication of what might be going on. I don't think anybody just looking at this scene in the early morning mist would know what is gliding by, but the sound of the oars tells everyone water is involved, and so it's quite likely people can formulate the image of a river and a boat [FIG. 4]. Maybe this is pure optimism and nobody knows what is happening; but I have never run into this as a question, and so I have a feeling that, at some level, it is working. In the second shot of the boat going by, it is much clearer that somebody is rowing—but what kind of boat is it? Nobody has ever seen this kind of boat. In the next shot of the prologue there is more pretty strange looking activity: the sand workers [FIG. 5] and then the little boy with his kite [FIG. 6]. They are there because I wanted the mystery to linger. The kite shot also introduces a visual element that is very important and will reappear throughout the film.

AÖ The boy almost runs into the sun here [FIG. 7].

RG Yes, what I was trying to suggest in the editing was that he was pulling the sun up. The idea is that the sun is being flown by the boy. I'm not so sure that works particularly well, but the kite takes on much more meaning as the film develops.

FIG. 7

ÁÓ Or the sun flies the boy. You see, there is a sense of "animism" in the film, a kind of preindustrial animism. You can feel this in the balance of nature, humanity, and divinity. One of the first things you encounter in Benares is the coexistence of vultures, dogs, kites, cows, and what not, together with the people and the river. There is no sharp division between these realms.

The bird/kite/river association is very strong. There was one occasion when we were on the river and there were these birds scavenging and creating this incredible tumult over the water. That shot is somewhere in the film, creating a mystery. I found this veritable churning of birds very telling, but I'm still not quite sure why.

FIG. 8

RG Well, I think that you certainly can appreciate the possibility of carrying over the burden of meaning in one film to another. I can't help thinking of the shots in *Dead Birds*. Also, I suppose, if it looks good and it seems to work, I just will not pass up a chance to put a bird in a film. Birds, for me, are wonderfully cinematic.

In the next shot of this prologue is another mysterious and very important visual element of the film, the steps [FIG. 8]. I'm sure, if we manage to keep talking, we'll be coming back to steps over and over again. Here is a shot that I can easily remember making because I was having such a difficult time getting something that I liked of those steps in the early morning at Manikarnika from the far shore. There is also in this scene some curious bundle lying on the steps. Now, I don't want anybody to be absolutely sure of what they're looking at here, but it is pretty clearly some ravens, and the bundle, as a matter of fact, is a human corpse wrapped and ready for cremation.

Next is a much closer shot of the boat gliding by, going in the same direction, down river [FIG. 9]. This is important because the whole thing reverses at the end of the film when the boats are going up river.

FIG. 9

FIG. 10

This following shot, of the sacred fire at Manikarnika, brings in the next element, fire [FIG. 10]. We have been talking about water and about mist or air and now we have, not unexpectedly, fire. The birds suggest air and the boats certainly suggest water. This fire is of a particular nature in that it is the holy fire needed for the cremations. Actually, I don't attach any particular significance to the fact that these three classic elements are all here in the film at this early stage. I had no thought in the editing that they should be. It has just happened that way. What is important is that certain visual motifs have appeared, like the boats, birds, dogs, kites, and steps. There may not be too many other visual elements of the same importance—except, of course, wood, bamboo, and also marigolds.

AÖ   The composition is very suggestive here, partly because it excludes the steps. In this shot they are not visible. But I see them even though they are not there. In anticipation of what's to come, I associate the steps with the fire.

RG   Well, maybe you can, but maybe nobody else can.

AÖ   Nobody else can. That's true. But on the steps there was this unnatural bundle; a bird flies through, and a boat comes with some bundles of its own, which are not moving. Then, as the boat leaves the frame, you see columns and the steps out of focus in the distance. Next is a close-up of the sacred fire where there ought not to be a fire; it is not where one normally encounters fire.

RG   I'm not thinking of it, as I've said, as one of the classic elements as much as one of the structural elements of the film itself. It is both, perhaps, if anyone wants it to be, but I never thought about it until this minute.

AÖ   I particularly like the sound of bells through this sequence, because it suggests peace. The river is the place of peace and quiet. Then there are quiet human noises, temple bells, and the creaking of oars. All these are coming through as ambiguous; we're not quite sure whether the bells are tolling for somebody.

RG   Exactly, exactly. I was just going to say that the bells are both merry and not so merry. They are meant to be full of the

possibility of delight and, equally, the possibility of sorrow.
I wanted some uncertainty to arise; that is precisely the mood
that is attempted here. Ambiguity plays such a prominent part
in creating an atmosphere. It is this mood that I hope continues
through the whole film until there is real clarity and the mysteries
get solved.

Sometimes I think, as I look at this and I talk to you this
way, that we are really out of our minds thinking all of this
is there. Really these are just pictures of some steps or of some
boat going by. Then along come some dogs that are just fighting
like dogs anywhere [FIG. 11]. I'm sure you
remember as well as I do that morning when
these dogs started fighting. We were on the
far side and I was trying to see Manikarnika
through the mist when, behind me,
I heard dogs snarling. Well, that tripped off
some reflex that spun me around and I
started shooting. Why it suddenly became
so important is hard for me, at this point,
to understand. I think it may have
epitomized one of the feelings I had about
Benares or perhaps about that side of the
river where bad things happen. This dogfight
becomes a very important image in the

FIG. 11

film. It does a great deal in terms of setting the tone and also
suggesting what the film is going to be about. This happens,
I suppose, because of its placement at the beginning of the film
and because of its brute strength as an image. I also had in
mind that it should serve to remind everyone the world is not the
best of all possible places to be; to survive, there is going to
be an awful lot of anguish to deal with, and sometimes you don't
quite make it.

ÁÖ   Yes, our boatman that morning laughed. First he thought it
was funny; then, after a while, he just broke the fight up.
On this occasion, nothing happened. In the film the scene acquires
a foreboding of sorts, partly, I think, because the scene fades out
before the rising sun appears. For me, this conjures up images of
the underworld, of sinking into the abyss, darkness. I know
that it disturbs people a great deal when they see this scene the
first time. I remember on this occasion—and many others when
we were filming such scenes—I was disturbed for reasons that
I still have to puzzle out, and maybe in this conversation I will.
While you were filming, I was really sensitive about the seemingly
negative aspects of the dogs, and you remember we had a lot of

discussion and arguments about filming the filth and the corpses, all these matters that outrage the uninformed visitor. It's not that one wants to deny these things and play into the hands of the superficial apologists for a "modern" India. Benares is not a hell-hole of death and corruption, but if certain people see any evidence for some of these things they will assume the basest motives for the images being included.

RG   I put the shot here hoping people will take note of it as almost a warning that they are going to see life unvarnished, unsparingly, and also so they will get the point I was making earlier that this is not the best of all possible worlds. I remember so well Luis Buñuel saying almost those exact words in answer to some question I had asked him about, I think, a sequence in his film *Los Olvidados*, or it might have been *Land Without Bread*.

ÁÖ   Apparently, I wasn't right in thinking this scene faded out. There is almost a sudden shift to black.

RG   Yes, I think we should go back because I don't think there are any optical effects there. I'm saying this because I had decided to use no effects anywhere in the film. I think the only place there is a dissolve is in the titles, and they were actually shot on the Oxberry animation camera. What you are thinking about is a simple scene change on a cut that takes you into something much darker. As you say, the sound continues over the cut and, that way, colors the next thing you see—which, in this case, is the quote from the Upanishads, translated by Yeats. Apart from the credits, this is the only appearance of words in the film. If the fighting-dogs image is a key to comprehending this film, so, in a way, is this quote, because it is as close as I've come to giving an explanation of what the film is about: "Everything in this world is eater or eaten, the seed is food and fire is eater." What I hope this is saying for people is that the nature of the world is such that things don't survive forever but, instead, are destroyed in any number of ways typified by burning or eating, and that then everything is brought forth again only to have the same thing happen over and over.

ÁÖ   Yes, this is a very rich reference. We talked about such things in Benares and even discussed specific verses from some of the sacred texts I was reading at the time. But I remember wondering in Benares what part words would play in the film, and we discussed this from time to time. I even remember reading out to you some verses from the Brihadaranyaka Upanishad with great enthusiasm. It wasn't this one. It was much longer, but it also had the cycle of the sacred fire and the soul going into the smoke to the Fathers, to the moon where it becomes food. Then it comes back to earth to be offered into the fire of man and woman. And so it moves in a circle.

RG   **I remember it seemed to me just a little too complex.**

AO   I know. But one of the ideas we discussed in Benares was that there might be a series of quotations, not just the one you opted for in the end. That way, the whole film would have been something of a dialogue, especially if the voice of the filmmaker could have been heard.

RG   **I remember that and even thinking of trying to use the person we called the "Poet" as an on-stage commentator, someone who might help us to somehow lyrically describe Benares in words. But this all vanished as a bad idea more or less the way the Poet himself dematerialized right after that strange afternoon of nightingale "wrestling."**

AO   That's right.

RG   **It always seemed problematic to me how anything from the heady and complex Hindu scriptural side of things could ever fit with the sort of images I wanted to have dominate the film.**

AO   But this is what is amazing, the way things fit into the film bringing both their deep Indian wisdom and their universality.

RG   **For me what is so appealing about the Yeats is that it brings you back to the English language.**

AO   Well, exactly. That's why you emphasize Yeats and not the Upanishads.

RG   **Right, I could have made the attribution in reverse order, putting the source first and the translator last.**

AO   And it is true that one could do this throughout the entire film. I could keep emphasizing the "Indianness" of everything and you could say that it belonged to the West and came from personal history and personal vision, and that would be true, too.

RG   Inevitably, inescapably, in a sense. We can't eliminate ourselves or India.

ÁÖ   Somehow, when this quotation appears here, it marks, in a way, the end of a preamble. And it says much in the way of summing up what's been seen until now and what will be seen later.

RG   It sums up, but it also foreshadows what's to follow. The sound is intended to be very suggestive through this part, especially now, when the present sound, of the dogs, gives way to another very important sound: that of trees being felled. Hopefully, that sound, too, has people wondering, not because they are disoriented but out of real mystification. I hope it calls to mind the idea of mature trees, anywhere in the world, being hacked down and falling in the forest. That, in turn, has its extended meaning in the well-known metaphor suggesting death, certainly the death of a tree if nothing else. I remember in a conversation with our friend Saraswati, early on in Benares, when I mentioned the idea I had of looking into the whole question of wood, his telling me about growing up in his childhood village and knowing that when he heard the sound of men cutting down the mango trees there had been a death. As far as the film is concerned, this sound will carry a pretty heavy meaning.

ÁÖ   Well, it comes from an actual forest outside Benares, and so it's absolutely authentic. It was a great deal of trouble to get to the forest; yet, in terms of the sound, any forest would have done.

RG   It is interesting. We went all that distance and looked and looked for something that would speak to the wood matter, and all I remember wanting was the sound of the tree coming down. Somehow the woodsmen themselves were too dwarfed by this metaphor coming out of what they were doing, and the whole chopping business just seemed puny. But when we heard the trees falling in the distance I realized that that was all we needed to have gone there for. I really think it would have been much less absorbing to see the tree being chopped down than just to hear it.

ÁÖ   You decided there and then that the visual aspect was unnecessary. I wondered why, since we were there, but it turned out that it would have been very different with that kind of literalness.

FIG. 12

RG   Exactly. So we were on the right track, or at least I hope we were on the right track.

And now, having been introduced by these eleven scenes conveying some of the most important elements to follow, the body of the film begins.

In contrast to the prologue, the main body of the film begins in a wholly different stylistic manner. It starts by examining one of the principal figures, Mithai Lal the Healer [FIG. 12]. It is early morning outside his house above Manikarnika, and my intention is simply to follow this man down to the river where he goes every morning for his ritual bath. Pictorially speaking, this is a very different way of making film than in the opening sequence of eleven shots, where each one is almost a film in itself or, at least, carries a tremendously important pictorial load. These early scenes of Mithai Lal are much more observational in character than the metaphorically loaded prologue sequence of eleven shots.

I remember this particular morning very well. It was when we waited for Mithai Lal to come out of his house, just as the sun was coming up, to go down and do something he did every day of his life. In a way, he's representing here many other Benarsies this morning. But he also is very much himself, and it's his wonderfully inimitable self that I was after almost more than anything else.

AÖ   There's no way of knowing who this man may be or turn out to be. It could be just a brief shot of somebody coming out of his house early in the morning. There's no indication that this is going to go on for a long time or that he's going to be a significant figure in the structure of the film.

RG   And one of the reasons we don't know any of this is that we haven't seen Mithai Lal before. But even more important is the fact that there is no narrator telling you what you should know about what you are looking at. There is nobody saying: "This is the Healer Mithai Lal, who gets up in his house in such a place and at such a time and starts down to the ghats for his morning bath in the Ganges." Again, the mystery is maintained to some extent, I hope. I think it's clear that at least the pictorial style has changed; it's leading people into another way of watching so that, hopefully, they are now going to be taken up by the narrative structure implicit in certain kinds of detail. What's being depicted is pretty routine, but at the same time there is something very idiosyncratic about how this old man gets himself about. At the end of these scenes there shouldn't be any real mystery about what you've been watching.

ÁÖ   There may be a little mystery in the untranslated greetings and bantering exchanged along the riverside. The lack of translation is an interesting thing, because here is one of the first places where people in the film are talking, and I'm sure some people watching it are waiting to be told what is being said. I'm also sure there are viewers who don't care. But this is one of the things that people who have seen the film have commented on. Essentially, audiences are divided in two: those who are frustrated by not being told anything, and those who enjoy finding their way by looking carefully at the images. Most viewers seem to tolerate the absence of narration in the prologue because it is so obviously a crafted assembly; however, past this opening sequence, some expect a voice to come on and help them out.

RG   Yes, people will think halfway through this sequence that either the voice track is faulty and they're not getting what they paid for, or that, in fact, it's never going to come. Maybe it's a crisis for the film here, where there still may be a large number of viewers who go on hoping for a voice-over that, as we know, never comes up on the track. Somehow the film has to beguile those who are waiting for the voice to forego it and just be content to watch.

There is plenty to say about any of these shots, and maybe that's what I should do from this privileged position we are in.

FIG. 13

The first thing to say is that this observing I'm doing of Mithai Lal is in fact directed at, among other things, the steps he's going down [FIG. 13]. So the sequence is about the fact that this man is going someplace and getting there thanks to the architectural device of steps. This picks up on the indications already made in the prologue, when stairs or steps were shown through the mist of early morning. There the intention was to suggest that steps had meaning beyond their functional purpose, that they were a transitional device for getting not just from one elevation to another but also from life to death. There's also the whole business of deliberate framing. There is a lot of very careful framing in the shooting of this film. If there weren't, there would be little hope of persuading anyone watching that they should be paying attention to something like these steps. I don't know whether we should be talking about these kinds of things or whether we should be on a loftier plane.

AÖ   No, I think this is fine, because this is how and where we are reminded of various things. Later on, we can decide if there was any value to the exercise.

RG   I'm reminded also that on this morning you were not with me.

AÖ   No, this particular morning I wasn't. I'm not sure where I was, maybe with Baidyanath Saraswati.

FIG. 14

RG   Well, this shot is framed to include not just a man walking down some steps but also a huge pile of wood which he is walking past. This framing is quite obviously deliberate, because it would have been much easier to position oneself so as only to be concerned with the man walking. But I wanted this wood in the frame because it is another important cinematic element in the development of the film's meaning. It comes early here, as it should. I can remember feeling almost a rush of excitement when I saw the wood as we were going down these steps with Mithai Lal. I remember also the weighing scales that were just sitting there at some landing, just waiting to be included in the frame with Mithai Lal [FIG. 14]. This wood is meant to be seen, and the camera can bring that intention off; in fact, it is almost the only thing that a camera can do. The reality of the wood is meant to be stored away in the viewer's head. No one knows yet quite why this wood is there. What is this wood anyway? It seems to be just wood, but maybe it's more than just wood.

AÖ   Now here again is the paradox of the simple passage. One can read all kinds of things into it. Is it or is it not really there? I'm not sure it matters. But, you know, an architectural feature such as stairs or gates, a constant passage through gates, doorways, and stairs—going up, going down, reversing direction and then eventually coming out at the river, past dogs, wood, and birds—

all makes for something very dense and rich, even though it's just a simple passing by of an old man going to his customary bath.

RG It would be interesting to know what meaning is actually lost by viewing a sequence in this manner. We can talk about these things with all kinds of certainty of their meaning to us, but then we were in Benares and we have had plenty of time to ponder it all. I have a feeling that fresh eyes watching this do assign significance to what the camera has taken pains to show them and that they are dealing with these elements, such as the steps, on other levels than as just paving stones that an old, grunting man descends. I might add that the grunting on the track at this point was not as apparent in actuality as it is in the film. The sound was deliberately enhanced in post-production.

AÖ But it was his grunting.

RG It was his, yes.

AÖ But not necessarily as he was going down the steps.

RG In fact, it was the sound he was making as he was going down the stairs. What I did was to change the balance and the intensity of the sound so that it really stood out. Very often when you're doing sound and image at the same time you don't get good sound quality. The image concerns are usually greater and, as a rule, take precedence. So we had to really work on the sound to bring it up and make it clear that Mithai Lal was not wholly enjoying this stretching of his arthritic limbs right after having gotten out of a warm bed.

AÖ But that groaning also establishes him. It's important that it is this man walking in this manner [FIG. 15]. It could have been someone else doing more or less the same thing in a completely mindless way. But, to me, when Mithai Lal eventually reaches the river and greets the sun, it is clear that he's been looking forward to it and is enthusiastic about it. He is not just a random individual desultorily making his way down some steps.

RG No, it's very purposeful.

AÖ And he has a kind of presence.

FIG. 15

RG   And these sounds and mannerisms with which he's getting himself there have, presumably, something to do with it. If everything is portrayed properly, the person is fleshed out as an individual. The camera can actually endow him with some personality or even some character.

AÖ   Rather than dealing with a type . . .

RG   Or average man.

AÖ   This could have been shot in a completely inconsequential way, just documenting what was happening. Maybe it's the framing, maybe it's the sound track.

RG   Or part of the impulse to do it in the first place.

AÖ   Or the time of day. In any case, it's not just reporting.

RG   That's right, and it's also correct that the manner in which the camera is used here is what fashions this event in a particular way. If I had been in front of Mithai Lal as he was coming down these steps, this sequence would have had a very different quality; it would have indicated immediately that he was entirely in complicity with the filmmaking and that he was being asked to stop and start as he was going down, because I would have had to run ahead to get the shot. There are all these implications depending on the angle of view of the camera, not to mention the point of view of the filmmaker. One of the facts in this situation is that I never asked Mithai Lal to stop or to go or sit down or repeat something. He just kept going down these steps to a place I had never even been.

   Maybe another question to ask at this point is whether the way the camera is being used to apprehend the actuality of Mithai Lal has any bearing on the realness or authenticity of what it shows. This question may have more relevance when the seemingly straightforward continuity of Mithai Lal's trip to the river's edge is broken by some intercuts. Quite suddenly and unexpectedly a pretty ordinary sequence is broken by an element, a pictorial element, which seems to have nothing sequentially to do with what we've been looking at for the last ten or fifteen shots. It is a sail going by [FIG. 16], but I wonder how many people

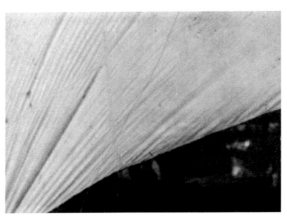

FIG. 16

FIG. 17

know this. It's hard for me to put myself in other people's heads, but I suspect there is a good deal of bewilderment, hopefully not too vexing, about what this is that goes by. What I wanted to do by introducing another recurring element in the film—the drifting past of boats—was to make the river become something more than a place to bathe.

On the track is the very important sound of dogs barking, and behind the sail are some vaguely discernible fires burning on the shore. I wanted people to say at this point: "My God, those are fires and those are dogs. What does it mean to be experiencing these things together here?" All anyone has been told is what is contained in the Yeats translation from the Upanishads, about the fire being eater and the seed being eaten. From what can be seen and heard in this scene of the sail going by, I doubt that anyone would know those are bodies that are burning on the shore. Then the scene shifts back to Mithai Lal and the observational present as against the metaphor of "sometime." All of the sounds are synchronous sounds; nothing has been added or even particularly enhanced. It's just the sound of a man going into the water. This is all very straightforward, stylistically speaking, until once again the continuity is interrupted by another, differently related image, not very easily explained, of an offering being made to the river [FIG. 17]—an offering of, what are these? Rice cakes . . .

ÁÖ   Sweets and flowers . . .

RG   There are saffron-colored marigolds on the larger leaf that's being put into the river as an offering. What this cut is meant to say is that just as the man is offering himself to the river, just as Mithai Lal is ritually bathing as an offering to the Goddess and to the sun, so is somebody else beseeching something with another kind of offering.

ÁÖ   Actually these are probably post-cremation funerary offerings.

RG   But I'm not trying to say anything like that at this point. All I really wanted with these shots was to suggest that people have many ways of dealing with heavy matters in their life and that this is a gesture of some significance that they are making.

ÁÖ   . . . also that, although the river is a river, it is also a goddess, that it's both a thing and something that transcends the thing.

<u>RG</u> **Yes, it gives and it takes.**

<u>AÖ</u> Mithai Lal being engulfed as he goes into the water with those gestures [FIG. 18] is a wonderful blend of spontaneity and gravity here, with the fire and the sail going past. Then we see him doing a little dance and, before the shot of the sail, he greets the sun with the other man on the riverbank. And then you see the offerings in the water intercut between shots of Mithai Lal swimming. Clearly all of this is in some way spontaneous. It just happens. And yet, you can read meaning into it.

FIG. 18

One of the things we will have to speculate about a little is how it happened that you ended up with the people who are in the film. At any time that could have changed or been different. It was always somewhat problematic. Where did the Dom Raja, Mithai Lal, or Ragul Pandit come from? Baidyanath or Omji led me to them, but these particular people need not have appeared in the film. Also, the filming at the burning ghats, at the temple, at all public places could have turned out badly, could have been stopped; but it kept going, from one difficult place to another. I still don't quite know why. And, you know, in the end many things didn't turn up in the film. I remember Saraswati had mapped out his agenda very clearly. And he was very important, to me at least. I spent a lot of time with him, especially towards the end when you were out shooting. I would be with him discussing things and thinking of what might be a part of the film. He often suggested that we ought to present the possibilities of Benares, which you could, if you wanted to, capture, mediate, or make real—a process that none of us quite understands but which is the whole magic of filming.

You know that many of the ideas I had didn't really fit into this film. It was clear halfway through that many of the death rituals which I thought should be in the film did not interest you. But, to me, the transition of the soul from ghost to ancestor and what people have to do to help this along—all that seemed to be a compelling and powerful process. Well, many of these things never ended up in the film, for obvious reasons. Others did; for example, Mithai Lal the Healer, whom Omji talked about so often. I remember not being particularly taken with the idea, for this film, having seen quite a number of healers. But Omji said that this one was different, and it turned out he was. We also thought this way about saddhus. Some are convincing and interesting, and others, for many different reasons, are not. You remember that you wanted to make a film about a saddhu and that the place to find one was in the mountains.

RG   **That would have been a much more tranquil undertaking.**

ÁÖ   When I went to Mithai Lal's house for the first time, I found him to be an extraordinary man. Then you and Chris James went with Omji to the Durga Temple on one of Mithai Lal's regular Tuesdays. It was fairly late in the game that Mithai Lal came into the picture, but your first reaction was that he had to be in the film. The fact that he agreed so readily was something of a surprise to you, I think.

RG   **Well, I think part of my enthusiasm for him was that he didn't look like he was going to be a very difficult subject, that he wasn't going to be temperamental and play a lot of time- and energy-consuming games. He was distinctly part of the vulgar world, and therefore had much less to protect in the way of an image. I think I was always intending that the film be about people who were quite real. I was never comfortable with the Sanskritists, as you must remember. But this does not really speak to your wonder that the film ever came together in such a problematic environment; and all I can say is that had Mithai Lal not come along someone else would have, and the film would not have been terribly different as a result.**

ÁÖ   One thing we very much wanted to get into was the world of the Dom Raja, and I recall our friends were not that keen on our pursuing it. I would have been equally disappointed had he not been a possibility, and I would have been disappointed had it not worked out with Mithai Lal or Ragul Pandit. These people are a great deal more to me than mere informants and characters in an anthropological field project. To me, they represent Benares in the best sense; something else would have come up, but it would have taken another couple of months and would have been different. In any case, there is something mysterious, something even uncanny about a character selection process like this one.

RG   **We are back to this initial sequence of Mithai Lal having a virtually real-time ritual bath in the Ganges [FIG. 19]. It is broken by intercuts that make pictorial comments on its actuality.**

FIG. 19

AÖ   This is so characteristic of Mithai Lal, a spontaneous little dance.

RG   I may already have said this, but here is a good example of a sequence intended to allow audiences to begin to orient themselves, to find their feet, in the "Geertzian" sense, with this new culture. Up until these images, through the first eleven shots, the viewer has had to work pretty hard. It has been both exciting and perplexing if it has been doing what it's supposed to do. Here, in the Mithai Lal introduction, things are relatively straightforward.

AÖ   Yes, that is very nice, that business about real time. It shows up the futility of legislating for film—saying what it should or has to do—because here an allegorical, even abstract, sequence is followed by real time without any conflict, the film form accommodating both.

FIG. 20

RG   Of course, the real-time sequence is not true real time because it is so telescoped, but it's continuous action. It is inflected from time to time by these intercuts. Here's one now of a dog gnawing on a decomposed corpse at the edge of the river [FIG. 20].

AÖ   It seems almost mummified.

RG   Well, I don't know what accounts for the chalkiness of that particular corpse, but this is where the idea of a world that is in constant, cyclical renewal is suggested by a pretty graphic image. It is one that, importantly, has a dog doing the devouring. This, you will recall, was already suggested by the early scenes of dogs in the prologue. As vivid as this image is, I think it's shot in a way that makes it difficult for most people to be sure that, in fact, it is a human corpse the dog is chewing on. I'm a little astonished when people don't know what it is, but that's because I was there and I could practically touch it.

AÖ   Then there is the sound of the oars.

RG   Yes, the oars—perhaps the most important sound in the film. Then comes this mysterious shot of the bow of a boat [FIG. 21]. We don't know who or what is in the boat or where it's

FIG. 21

FIG. 22

FIG. 23

going; it's simply on its way. And then we go back into the more or less real-time sequence of Mithai Lal as he completes his offerings to the Goddess.

AÖ   It ought to be clear by now that he is engaged in a devotional task. There have been so many indications that what he is doing is making offerings [FIG. 22]: for example, saying "Ma, Ma" (Mother, Mother), which is hardly the usual utterance while taking a mere swim.

RG   So the whole thing is ritual.

AÖ   Yes, and it is something that is not rote or "mere" ritual. He is inventing the ritual as he goes. It's a world with which he is entirely familiar, and all these gestures suggest that. When he is doing that little dance, when he is pouring the water, he is combining personal with conventional ritual. He is just a superb performer, not for the camera but for the . . .

RG   . . . for the culture?

AÖ   Yes, yes, and for his wife, his friends, and for the Goddess. He is always in the presence of the Goddess.

RG   We have cut to the Dom Raja's house now, and the idea behind this cut, which is to the big bell being rung there [FIG. 23], is to parallel Mithai Lal's little ceremony and suggest that worship is simultaneously going on somewhere else in the city. This act of ringing the bell is also meant to have about the same weight as Mithai Lal's devotional gestures. As it turns out, the Dom Raja stands, along with Mithai Lal and the soon-to-be introduced Ragul Pandit, as one of the three most prominent figures in the film. I want also here to indicate that, as in the case of Mithai Lal's ritual bath, the scenes concerning the Dom Raja are taking place just above and alongside the river. I don't know how I thought I could be sure the audience would recognize this, but I'm confident that at a certain point in the film there is little doubt concerning the location of the Dom Raja's house. Something else to note is that the style of shooting here—observational but including sounds extrinsic to the actual scenes—is also similar to the Mithai Lal sequence. In the case of the Dom Raja sequence I also heightened the sound, especially of dogs and of birds.

ÁÖ   And the Dom Raja is in a way set up as much by Mithai Lal's worship at the river as by the birds circling above those tigers

FIG. 24

[FIG. 24]. This is an amazing little vignette right at the beginning. It is significant that you were actually shooting at this time, that you were expecting something to happen. There wasn't much happening, and most of the time we were just waiting for him to make up his mind about us and about what he was going to do next.

RG   I remember this particular time I was just waiting for him to wake up or sober up.

ÁÖ   Or whatever, but I suppose you may have been taking a chance hoping something would happen.

FIG. 25

RG   I wonder if it is ever as simple as that. I think after a certain amount of experience in this world of nonfiction filmmaking a kind of seeing and knowing develops that tells you something is about to happen. I don't completely understand this process, but I am sure there are some signs, some subtle indications that form a pattern alerting you to the fact that something important is in the air. On this particular day, I was shooting the Dom Raja while he was asleep [FIG. 25]. I was also sensing that he was going to wake up and that that change and how it unfolded would be interesting. As it turned out, it was more than just interesting, and there certainly would have been no way for me to stop the camera once I saw what was happening through the lens. These are relatively rare experiences, at least for me, and they are very trancelike when they happen. It's impossible to resist the urgency of the experience. I would guess that one of the ways an argument might be made that this kind of filmmaking has some art to it is to develop the idea of there being a sensitivity to the way things unfold in actuality. How much this is a talent and how much it is simply craft gained through long experience in observing life is hard to answer, but that there are people who anticipate and others who don't is pretty easy to tell just by looking at a reasonably wide sample of nonfiction films. I would think that lacking any sense of how the world you try to enter as a filmmaker evolves or develops would be extremely frustrating. Not being able to anticipate puts the actuality filmmaker at a terrible disadvantage because there is no way to keep that critical, anticipatory instant ahead of what's happening without such an ability. But again, many films do suggest either that the filmmaker was there after it happened or that the scene was contrived for the benefit of the camera.

AÖ   Is it possible to begin filming with this kind of anticipation but then have to stop because nothing happens, leaving you with no choice but to simply abandon the shot?

RG   There's a strange feeling that comes over you, I think, as you're looking through a camera at something you think is going to be really compelling. It hasn't happened yet; it's going to happen you're told by some occult knowledge, and you're riveted, absolutely riveted. It's impossible to shut down because your hand cannot go near the switch. But, as I've said, this is rare. It probably happened only ten times during the whole ten weeks I was shooting in Benares. When it does happen, though, you know you're onto something. I can remember thinking, "My God, you know this is as close to cinematic orgasm as I'll get." You're at the height of your power, at the height of your ecstasy as a filmmaker. It's a strange, strange thing I'd like to think about more. But here is the third major figure, Ragul Pandit, brought in by that familiar device of parallel editing. It is early morning and it is also on the river [FIG. 26].

AÖ   I had a feeling about these three people. I especially hoped that Ragul Pandit would be a part of the film. It was never clear that he would be as pivotal as the other two. He is certainly less recognizable, at least initially. People may later on associate him with the ending; but, you know, the fact is he is so much a part of Dasashwamedh Ghat, and he is

FIG. 26

so utterly convincing as a ritualist and worshiper of the river. I don't think this could be lost on anyone.

RG   We are at a place in the film, Ákos, where the third important figure, Ragul Pandit, is seen for the first time. He is seen in what we have been calling an observational manner. Here, Ragul is beginning his morning worship at the edge of the Ganges.

The three main figures are never portrayed in any depth. In fact, they are never even named. But they do get sufficient attention to emerge as fairly well-rounded individuals. So this is Ragul Pandit, and he's down at the river. Let's just look and see if there's anything particular to be said about it beyond the fact that it is important for this introduction to take place at the river, as in the case of Mithai Lal and the Dom Raja.

It was always clear to me the film would take place in the pretty limited physical setting that included the two shores and the river in between. Of course, there are a few scenes outside this locale, such as those in the interior gullies and in Sarnath, outside the city proper. But the majority of scenes are on the ghats or on the river itself. This was one of the ways I had hoped to simplify things in order to reduce the enormity of the chaos.

ÁÖ   This is an almost real-time sequence of a man doing a daily ritual. Again, you shot the scene from the shore without getting a point of view from the river. Was there any reason for this, or did it just seem to be an appropriate parallel to the way the other main figures were filmed? I'm not sure whether this was done at about the same time as Mithai Lal's walk. It was also fairly late in the morning, later than Ragulji would customarily be doing this kind of worship. It is after the sun has risen.

RG   Yes, I couldn't do anything before the sun had started to appear on the horizon. There just wouldn't have been enough light to make an exposure without artificial lights. As to when in our stay it was shot, I'm sure this all happened after the midpoint.

ÁÖ   Yes, it was done rather late because these shots were, in a way, planned. These were things, I remember, that you intended to film at some convenient point. They could be done any time because they were virtually daily occurrences.

RG   As I've mentioned, this sequence was shot under the constraints of the physical situation we were all in—the crowded steps and the river full of boats and people. I stayed on the steps rather than walking out into the river or jumping into a boat. Part of the reasoning behind this choice, as I recall, was that there was no way to get into the river without losing a great deal of the action. What Ragul Pandit was doing would have been seriously altered if I had asked him to wait while I found a boat to get nearer or to get on the river side of him. The whole mood and quality would have changed quite drastically. So the true tempo was preserved by observing from the shore only. As I speak about these things, I realize that a close look at my films would probably show this is the way I usually do things and that, as a result, I am often following what is happening.

AÖ   This is a detailed little film within the film, and so was the first sequence with Mithai Lal. They are parallel, in a way: just two characters involved in two ritual activities that are repeated daily. It is very ethnographic.

RG   Well, yes, I guess if there is anything ethnographic about the film it is to be especially seen in these kinds of sequences.
     What concerned me as this was being shot and then, later, as it was being edited was whether it could help orient people in relation to this locale that I've already mentioned, the river and its two shores. I'm also interested in establishing the idea of it being early morning. The film has the structure of a complete day. This is part of the key notion I wanted to plant in people's minds: that the film starts with the sun rising, actually being pulled up by that boy who's flying a kite. Next is Mithai Lal, who gets up and comes down to the river, and the Dom Raja, who wakes up. These could be afternoon events, I suppose, but I think there really is a kind of morning quality to them.
     Now, as you see, we are back with Mithai Lal after an interlude with the Dom Raja and Ragul Pandit, and this means Mithai Lal is the most important of the three, at least for now, because I'm spending more time with him. It's also cut this way because the material I shot on him doing this devotional business with the lingams and other idols seems to work best at this point in the film.

AÖ   Well, this is another lighthearted sequence and would seem to be quite immaterial to the whole film. Yet, in a way, it is quite central, because here he is actually saying what the image alone had to establish up till now: namely, the business about how hard it is for him to move his bones and how the fact that he can even dance is due to the goodness and power of the Goddess. None of this is translated, of course, but some people do speak Hindi, and that bit of conversation is important to them. However, I have discovered that even people who are fluent in Hindi realize that these conversations are not significant. But they can't help understanding what is being said in the conversation.

RG   **That's the thing with words. When you hear them or see them, the mind has to grasp their literal meaning, at first at least.**

FIG. 27

AÖ   . . . hear them and then realize at a certain point they don't matter. But in this particular case the words are telling you what the images are showing you. The scene shows him addressing the river as Goddess [FIG. 27], and then he says, in reply to some question, that it's the Goddess who makes it possible for him to dance. This fascinates me, because it's not important in watching the film that you know any of this. But the fact that he is there, and that his gestures visually express exactly what he means, makes the event into something ordinary, everyday, and also transcendent. The fact that you may know, or that somebody tells you, he is saying the Goddess is making him dance is an interesting dimension that is not particularly necessary; but, in another sense, it is quite important because it's just the right thing to be hearing here. So, again, this interplay of subjectivity and the given world that may be unnecessary for the structure of the film seems, to me, to deepen the experience of the film by allowing one to see the river as Goddess and to realize the importance of the relation between Mithai Lal and his Goddess.

RG   **On the other hand, if you were to elect to put into subtitles a translation of what he was saying about the Goddess making him dance, I don't think it would materially add to your comprehension.**

AÖ   It would confuse and distract. Sometimes, when the dialogue is unintelligible, subtitles are used to clarify things; but instead they distract. Subtitles would ruin the effect because they would only raise questions about the film and would not be able to emphasize the river as Goddess. You don't want people asking, "Why am I being asked to read subtitles?"

RG   **Or, "Why am I being told this at this point, and can I really rely on whoever is putting up those words, that that is in fact what is being said?"**

FIG. 28

In this sequence of Mithai Lal returning to his house, the sound is pretty straightforward. What you hear is pretty much what was happening. No sounds have been removed or added until we get to this stairway, where his footsteps and his groans are once again enhanced for emphasis. It was my hope when shooting this that the audience would recognize this stairway as being the same one that he used to come down, and that he was going to go back through the same portal through which he came earlier [FIG. 28].

In the foreground is a pile of dung-colored material that looks to be of suspiciously human origin. I recall with great clarity making this shot. I remember as I was following him up the first flight of steps above the river that the sun had come up high enough to feel pretty warm, that I was quite weary from the effort already made, and that a substantial part of my remaining energy and vigilance had to go into avoiding little mounds of human excrement deposited on these steps earlier in the morning. I was thinking, "My God, this really is pretty hard on one's sensibilities this early in the morning." You not only have to think about trying to make a beautiful film but to wonder when some human waste is going to be squeezed up between your toes as you take your next step. So I decided there was only one way to deal with this, and that was to include it in the film. And I remember framing that neat little dropping to let people know this film was going to be different from *Passage to India* or *Jewel in the Crown*. It is still amazing to me that such films, and others that strain even harder to achieve realism, never show anything as ordinary or as innocent as someone taking a pee.

AÖ   There is a question about that. Given the tremendous hardships sustained while making this film, these things were potentially upsetting. I remember you asking if I really didn't notice these things. I may have just edited them out, and you asked me a number of times: "Doesn't it bother you?" At one point you said: "I honestly think that you don't see these things anymore." That may be what happens in the film when you say that a particular pile of shit is no longer hideous and that many people don't even notice what it is. These things are certainly a part of Benares, but, on the other hand, if that's where one stops then one never gets to the river, and never reaches the transcending part of it. It is a part, it's there, it's noted.

RG Now it's at this point, on the other side of that portal—where we come upon Mithai Lal stopping to give alms to some beggars—that the sound track begins to include more than what was there. What has been added is the sound of wood being split by big sledgehammers into burnable logs. It's here I thought people should begin to wonder about that sound. It comes into prominence and joins other major sounds—the oars creaking and dogs barking. This sound of wood being split is a key sound.

ÁÓ Yes, this may have been enhanced or even added to, but, as I remember, you can actually hear wood being split here.

FIG. 29

RG Right, there is every reason to hear it here. Absolutely. This is just above Manikarnika Ghat, and it is likely that at this time in the morning plenty of wood is being split. The thing is that if it were not emphasized you might easily not register it as a discrete and telling sound. Here, it seems to me, is one of the unfortunate paradoxes of cinéma vérité. So often the sound taken while shooting in that style is frequently not at all true. It often is just barely audible and is having a hard time competing at some low decibel level with the inherent noise of the tape recorder or the projector. Anyway, here we go back up these stairs, and this is all fairly straightforward, including the sleeping body in the stairwell [FIG. 29], which I remember hoping would resonate with the shot in the prologue of the bundled-up corpse seen from the far shore.

ÁÓ Which is motionless at first, and then you realize . . .

RG It comes to life. And then more of Mithai Lal's religious undertakings, more ritual gestures.

ÁÓ Well, this sequence I was particularly happy about. I wasn't there that morning. We had talked a lot about the lingams of Shiva and how the whole locality of Benares was aptly described in the texts as a forest of lingams. Shiva is known to have said that about Benares because so many of his lingams are there. But the very notion of a lingam is so abstract and yet so palpable and real in its connection with the generation of life. So it is at once very earthy and immediate, and also difficult and abstract. It is hard to imagine for outsiders how all this is made real as an object of veneration or as an idea of a great civilization. Benares is very much tied up with this idea, and I suspect it is not particularly cinematic.

RG   Right, it's not even particularly accessible, it would seem, on a conceptual level.

ÁÖ   Exactly. And yet the ideas we've just described are unmistakably in the film and emerge here partly, I suspect, because Mithai Lal is treating these objects with veneration. Whether people understand that he's calling them Father (Baba) doesn't matter. What must be obvious is that he is having some kind of interior encounter with them while he adorns them and pours water on them [FIG. 30]. I'm confident these things are grasped immediately at an intuitive level. The viewer will have to look outside the film for conceptual satisfaction.

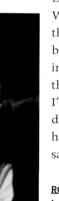

FIG. 30

RG   But that kind of satisfaction might be a long way off if the viewer is asking for the whole doctrinal or metaphysical background of the thing. I suppose it could be said that these images are an attempt at a sort of first-level explanation of what people who are praying look like.

ÁÖ   Pouring water is one of the most basic gestures of Hindu worship, and it's done so naturally here that you have to believe this is a sacred act.

FIG. 31

RG   I should say something about this next shot, where he is just walking along and the camera hesitates on a kite lying in the street. I remember this well. I saw the kite out of the corner of my eye and knew that it could play a part in heightening an awareness I wanted attached to kites. By this time, I had already spent quite a bit of time trying to get useful kite shots down on the ghats. Here was a kite that evoked a somewhat different mood, lying, as it did, rather forlornly in the dust [FIG. 31]. I might wish that I had held a count or two longer on the kite at the end of the shot, but I think it serves as intended because people often cite this shot as a key to their understanding of how the film works. Here again is an example, I think, of how nonfiction filmmaking is more than luck, more than an artifact of actuality. It has the possibility, at least, to shape a vision out of a distinct and particular awareness of actuality.

Here I was following Mithai Lal back to his house. That was my immediate task; but at some other level of intention I'm looking for something that in reality might be nothing more than a piece of color, a ragged, old, fallen-down kite. The shot isn't consummately well made, but at least it takes one's eye to an object that will be of some importance later on. So we, and Mithai Lal, go on. Here is some pretty routine religious gesturing, I suspect.

AÖ   Yet he's almost caressing these stone images.

RG   This is the first cow, isn't it? For us it is not so easy to tell, because there is nothing remarkable about seeing one just standing and munching away like this in the street. But for anyone who doesn't know India, seeing a cow in everyone's way, just doing as it pleases, is pretty amazing. It also can be pretty problematic for the filmmaker.

The camera is deliberately centered through this particular passage on Mithai Lal's feet and where he is putting them, especially the steps. This is the last shot of the sequence, I think, and it's where he walks away from the camera and disappears into a little alleyway [FIG. 32], presumably to go back into his house.

FIG. 32

What is important about it is that it marks the end of a distinct part of the film. On the track we hear the sound of wood being split to remind us there is considerable mystery left to work out.

This initial phase of the film is meant to introduce first, in the prologue, the central themes of the film, and second, in the first observational sequence, the three figures who will stand out in the larger human landscape. The next phase of the film opens in this wonderfully peaceful field of marigolds out in Sarnath. There is nothing in the film to tell us where it is, but maybe people can feel a little of the relief we ourselves felt when we found it. Here also is a new element: the simple marigold. Going after this flower has a great deal of quite specific intention behind it. This is not just a pretty landscape in which people might find a little serenity; it is the source of an item that is supposed to bring us all closer to knowing what it feels like to

MAKING FOREST OF BLISS

FIG. 33

be in the culture. Admittedly, this item, the lowly marigold, is pretty frail and slender [FIG. 33]. But, as we have often discussed before, Ákos, film seems to work best with simple motifs, with commonplaces. To escape the difficulty awaiting anyone who tries to film complexity as complexity and then maybe tries to explain their way out of these complexities in subtitles or voice-over, the idea in this film was to look for some quite ordinary realities, such as dogs, wood, kites, marigolds, etc., and to plunge into them, trusting that they will provide an evocative journey into their meaning.

ÁÖ   That's very important, because I remember my whole focus at the beginning was much more on the ritual process than on objects. I would only look at objects in their symbolic dimension. What interested me as we did more filming is that people like Mithai Lal and Ragul Pandit, who had an acquaintance with the town and who were practicing ritualists, might offer something to the film, and the film might offer something to the town. This other "commonplaces" business was a bit of a surprise to me, because at that point I didn't conceive of it as a possibility. Having seen it and having thought about it in terms of the film, I don't quite know how to explain it except to say that it works. I under-stood the idea at the time the film was being made, but I still remember my surprise when you first mentioned wanting to work with things like marigolds. Now, of course, it makes sense. You can embrace so much of Benares in this way. But I did originally doubt that this might be a way of creating a thread with which to connect these other complexities, which, as you mention, are so totally incomprehensible by themselves. Perhaps you could have used such a thread through a whole bunch of rituals. That might have been a solution, although I remember that you felt the ritual elements were too tiny and too . . .

RG   . . . too many . . .

ÁÖ   . . . too many and too detailed . . .

RG   . . . too esoteric and too cerebral.

ÁÖ   What has been done is to create a story about the marigolds, and about the wood and the dogs and so forth. One sees the flowers used in various ways: on people, on corpses, on deities, etc. Then within the film, or maybe just because it is film, you get the symbolic or metaphorical side, too.

RG   It should be mentioned that this idea or solution really came out of some very real desperation. As an observer who regards the city as having endless possibilities for confusion, I was no different from anyone else living in Benares. Here was a city of institutionalized chaos—and what can you do with chaos? I mean, you can only represent chaos. Perhaps it's the ideal topic for cinéma vérité. It's hard to take it apart and see what is going on or what is meaningful about it. Photographed, it just becomes visual noise, and the only way I could see to get away from the visual noise of Benares was to find refuge, almost literally, in the marigolds or the wood or something extremely simple yet somehow charged. The fact these so-called simple things exist and take their meaning from this world, this chaotic world, meant that world would be drawn in by implication. Had I tried to deal with the world itself or even large parts of it, I think we would all have gone mad. I certainly would have when I got home and saw it in the rushes.

AÖ   I wonder, though, whether you knew when you decided on the marigold theme what it would look like in the finished film.

RG   Well, no, because that kind of thing isn't really ever clear until the editing. What I was doing in Benares was just trying to keep the confusion level lower by using some device to reduce the sense of chaos I felt every time I woke up.

AÖ   What interests me is how this all came together. Was it the power of Benares or of filmmaking? What I'm getting at is that the structural import of this whole process could not have been foreseen. The intuitive approach may have been to make sense out of disorder, but the structural significance of the devices in this film must have been born on the editing table.

RG   Well, in its final form, yes; but in its intention, it was certainly born in Benares.

AÖ   The marigolds' potential was always there—the marigold images could parallel those of the wood, the boat, etc.—but somehow they became so much more because of their presence throughout the film.

FIG. 34

FIG. 35

RG Of course, the placement of this marigold passage here, after the Mithai Lal sequence, is to some extent arbitrary. I actually think it was done partly for the sake of the light in that I was trying to sustain the notion of a day passing; but I also put it here because I wanted another quiet passage before getting swept away by the din and clatter of Benares. It turned out that, while keeping faith with Benares, I avoided, as much as possible, filming that din.

These shots showing marigolds being brought into the city from the fields are ways of trying to burn the color of marigolds into people's minds. And now, right next to this very quiet sequence, comes a bit of din and clatter. It is loud, raucous, hard work by men taking wood that has been brought in by train and trucks down to a boat that will ferry it up to the cremation ground. Once again, in terms of style, this sequence is quite conventionally shot. It, too, is observational, I suppose. But what is slightly peculiar is that the sequence is so long for what it is. Why spend this kind of screen time on men carrying great loads of wood on their heads [FIG. 34] down to a huge barge into which they are dumped [FIG. 35]? There is the pretty obvious intention of creating a little tension in the form of a mystery or question about what this wood is for.

ÁÖ It just struck me that the audience is seeing and hearing what is actually happening as these additional "characters" are being introduced. I mean, just as with Mithai Lal, Ragul Pandit, and the Dom Raja, here we have marigolds and wood, which are also characters, in a sense.

RG Yes, very much so. They definitely end up playing roles, and I hope that people watching the film are concerned with what happens to them, just as they would be with a person.

ÁÖ The barge almost capsized there.

RG Well, everything is almost capsizing in Benares, isn't it? The sound the wood is making is something that I want people

FIG. 36

FIG. 37

FIG. 38

to make central to their auditory life at this point. They will become more and more familiar with it as time goes by. The next shot, of the barge shoving off upstream with the load of wood [FIG. 36], is followed by a scene of birds circling over the river [FIG. 37]. I think you called it a "turmoil of birds" above the river, and it was shot more than anything else for its cinematic beauty or richness. Right after the birds is a shot of a corpse in the water [FIG. 38], unmistakable for what it is, unlike the first corpse, in the prologue. Now these two shots, the birds and the corpse, are connected by editing, not at all by actuality. Still, the birds are as incredibly actual as the corpse, and, of course, spliced together they're making the usual A + B = C. The corpse and the birds are put in here, when the wood is on its way up river to Manikarnika, in order to say that wood has some death-related meaning, that it is not just for keeping people warm at night. I would hope all this is fairly clear from the editing.

The next cut is back to Mithai Lal in his house. You and I have no trouble knowing this is Mithai Lal, the person last seen as he went into the alleyway near his house. We also have no trouble knowing that he is in his own house. But the audience is not so privileged. There are no subtitles such as "In Mithai Lal the Healer's House," or any commentary. So there is perhaps more mystery than I want. There may even be some perplexity, which I definitely don't want. But I saw no solution other than pressing on with hope and confidence in the material and the audience. Surely there is no question what is happening in this house. Even if one wonders whose house it is or even who it is in the house, one will know that religious things are happening. The fact that it is not easy to see that the individual disappearing in an alleyway is the one who makes religious gestures in a dimly lit house in front of household deities means that nonfiction film may have problems as a narrative genre.

ÁÖ   That may be. But I think there is an even greater worry about this nonfiction format. At the end of the film, when the viewer has seen the last of Mithai Lal, what is it that comes through of his life? Here the nonfiction film, curiously enough, hasn't represented so much as it has evoked. In a way, I think people would come closest to getting an "accurate" rendering with Ragul Pandit, obviously a ritualist or priest of sorts and always seen as such in the film. But as far as recognition goes, is Ragulji at the end the same man as at the beginning? Do people pick that up? I think everyone picks up that the man who was being massaged is the one who screams at people at Manikarnika Ghat.

RG   Yes, there's less of an identity problem with the Dom Raja. It may be his utter balefulness that gives him such distinction. It may also be that just because everyone will not necessarily know it is Mithai Lal every time he pops up in a new context, the film is not irreparably damaged. Something is being done by someone, even if we don't know his name or that he is the same person we saw in another sequence. And if whatever is being done is reasonably compelling, even if only in a graphic sense, then it will tell us something even though nobody is being developed as a character in the familiar, narrative sense.

ÁÖ   In a similar vein, it's possible to regard these as six, or eight, or ten different people, according to however many times they enter the film. This does not seriously undermine the enterprise, because even if people regard each of your main figures as multiple persons, one walking and the other worshiping and so on, they are still of a piece, all parts of the same puzzle. They are different aspects, almost different manifestations of the same person. It's not an alien notion that we have one person with . . .

RG   Several personas?

FIG. 39

ÁÖ   Here it seems to me entirely obvious that what he's doing is worshipping [FIG. 39]. This is probably clear to everyone, but it's also a form of reaching out and striving that is going on. Even in his gestures, he's trying to connect in some way.

RG   He is reaching out. But this is our speculation on the basis of not so much evidence on the screen. We have much more evidence gathered in visits and conversations that are not filmed that this is what he's doing. So the speculation is pretty well informed, and it may be as close as anyone can get, at least by looking at it in images, to the phenomenon of reaching out.

If I had an actor and directed him to pray in such a way that he was showing a desire to reach out to another human being, it might not be as successful or convincing. It certainly would be different. On this score, I think that the concern I've been expressing about nonfiction limitations has something to do with worries that are fairly personal, and I really don't mean to suggest that the nonfiction form is bankrupt. It would be nice for people to understand that it is the same person in scene #1 as it was in scene #2, but maybe as much for reasons of keeping things more simple and tidy as anything else. It's also appealing to be able to keep things personalized as to identity. This is so easy in fiction because individuals are always calling each other by name. It's interesting to me that I personalized in this way twenty-five years ago by using names in *Dead Birds,* but in this film I haven't recognized anyone by name except Yeats.

FIG. 40

Getting back to this sequence of Mithai Lal in his house, I should say that I remember worrying, when I was editing, about whether to allow this long interlude to continue, whether it was taking up too much screen time. He's blowing a conch shell [FIG. 40], but why does he have to blow it three times? Why not just let him blow it once and get on with something else? This is a really interesting problem, especially for you, Ákos. When are the requirements of film going to overrule the requirements of fidelity, and vice versa? Matters of rhythm and pace are not inconsequential.

AÖ   I remember thinking about this and recall feeling that if he blows the shell once, he has to blow it three times. Because that's how he looks at it.

RG   He would never blow it once?

AÖ   No, never. But for the sake of a film, somebody might justify that in this particular instance he would blow it only once. Maybe that makes sense in some way, but then there is the other question (and it's a very important question) of whether you should or even can count on a necessary lack of familiarity on the part of the audience. Would that unfamiliarity be the only thing to allow such abbreviation? If you feel that this man is fulfilling a cultural and individual intention, then there is just no way that he can do anything but blow three times. So here it was definitely justified to let him do so, even if it drags out the scene, because it would be so uncharacteristic for him to do otherwise. Only a person unfamiliar with the worship would raise no objection.

RG   **Would permit one blow?**

ÁÖ   Yes, such a viewer would just accept it.

RG   **But that is virtually everyone who will look at the film.**

ÁÖ   Except the Indian viewer, and yes, except yourself, who knows that no worship is complete without sounding the conch shell three times.

RG   **Myself and also his "self," at least to the extent I present one. Here, as anywhere else where we represent someone, there is a great risk that it will be done badly or insufficiently. But now I think I'm getting into the question of maintaining, among other things, an individual's dignity in the process of representation. What happens to dignity if what is shown is not what happened or is only part of what happened? My view is that probity is the issue, but that it is not a simple question of whether some rendering in images is or is not a faithful reproduction. It is entirely possible, if not likely, that the most brief and telling view of someone will be the one that best assures the preservation of dignity. I think, in this regard, that much has also to do with the grace of the action within the image and also the grace with which the action itself has been filmed. In this sequence, Mithai Lal unburdens himself of an enormous belch. I really didn't hesitate to include that when editing. Why hasn't it diminished his dignity? Could it have anything to do with the way it was shot? The way it was graphically delivered? That there is a context already provided within which to deal with this event? I also have included in this sequence the part of his worship in which he bangs his head on the stone floor very hard three times [FIG. 41]. I even enhanced that sound in order to let people know that it could hurt. Does this compromise or enlarge his dignity?**

FIG. 41

AÖ   These things are all so much a part of his worship. There are many considerations, including being truthful to the man, to oneself, to the situation. Then there are the aesthetic concerns of where this sequence goes in relation to the whole and how it relates to the other parts. I can't see that there are any absolute rules. There are some moments where you almost intuitively feel that something is ethically just.

RG   I'm put in mind of that Goethe quote you like so much, where he says things have to be legal or lawful and harmonious.

AÖ   Yes, art's responsibility is to the lawfulness, harmony, proportion, and passion of things. In our case, this brings up a major point of distinction, that between the lawfulness of the ritual and its integrity and the integrity of this work of art in which the ritual finds itself. These are not the same thing, yet they have to coexist as governing principles. I don't mean that they have to be isomorphic or parallel but that they have to be taken into account. I found with the Bengal films that the structure of the ritual is not necessarily the structure of the film. The verbal story is not the same as the visual story. Sometimes these things are working against each other. There is no reason or rule that everything has to be cinematically or verbally solvable. I find that trying to write a narrative of a ritual is an almost impossible task—that is, without taxing the reader's attention. It's an exacting task, in which film's narrative genius puts it at a great advantage; but even film has its problems in that it does not merely record reality. It presents an image or model—in other words, an invention of reality. This is perhaps more powerful than the real thing because within the space of a few seconds it may have to suggest several hours.

RG   We now have come to the end of this sequence of Mithai Lal in his house, and it ends, as I've mentioned, with him banging his head quite hard. This took me totally by surprise; in fact, I think I missed the first bang because I was so unprepared for it. I was impressed. I truly felt that I had witnessed a person of enormous faith and desire. So the shot stayed in with the risk that it is seen as bizarre. This is a dilemma but not insurmountable, it seems to me. Bizarre behavior is still behavior, and I think it is true that we all learn more quickly from it than from conventional behavior. This is true, however, only if there is a context for this "exaggerated" life. It's easy to imagine a simply exploitative approach showing the outrageous for the sake of outrage. But I'm thinking of the kind of examination of human behavior that falls more into the surrealist realm. What I'm talking about can be seen in Werner Herzog's *Land of Silence and Darkness,* for example. You remember, I'm sure, the profoundly moving deaf mutes who, while showing us some pretty antic behavior, really do speak to the experience of silence and darkness.

AÓ   That's an interesting cut from the marigolds on the Goddess.

RG   So you saw exactly what was intended. There are plenty of montage theories, but I suspect they all deal with this rather simple cutting on an object, from the marigolds on the idol to them being strung into garlands. The shooting here has something to be said about it. There doesn't seem to be that

FIG. 42

much going on: some ladies in the courtyard of their house putting blossoms on strings. But there is a bed with a bundle, actually a sleeping baby, in the foreground of the long shot [FIG. 42]. Obviously, it took a conscious act of choice to frame the scene that way. It would have been much easier and far more direct to come in closer and be on the flowers side of the bed, just shooting what the ladies are doing. By putting the sleeping, motionless child in the foreground, some-thing more than straight documentary intention is suggested. For me, the baby was a source of tension; would it wake or sleep, would it live or die? The garlands will be used in various ways throughout the film, not least of all as offerings on dead bodies. What I'm saying is that the sleeping figure is being used to indicate the ambiguity of sleep. It's not simple sleep but the possibility of permanent sleep, of death, that is being filmed. There is another element that is being put into the play of montage here, and that is the dog. Here is a puppy [FIG. 43], parallel with the sleeping baby but nonethe-less a dog, that is very busily engaged with the motif of the marigolds. The dog playing with them reveals that there is a light side

FIG. 43

to being a dog, to marigolds, and even to life itself. This whole sequence has several intended redemptive qualities.

There is a cut now to a traveling shot on the river from a boat moving upstream past some pretty typical shoreline activi-ties, including a figure squatting at what we came to call the "shitting ghat" [FIG. 44]. It is quite a small figure, and I don't think everyone will know why he is squatting—which hardly matters since the intent is to supply atmosphere only.

FIG. 44

AO   As the camera moves past the sandboats, there is a fleeting and telling glimpse of a man circumambulating the big lingam at Harishchandra Ghat.

RG   Indeed. When I made that shot I had no idea he was there. I didn't see him until well into the editing. This was a strange thing for me, because I usually see everything in a frame. It was almost as if he came into the image after I had made the shot. Anyway, it goes to show how thick some of this "Geertzian" description can get.

AO   I like it. So many things are happening in that brief passage on the river bank, on the ghats.

FIG. 45

FIG. 46

RG   Now the life cycle of the marigold continues as it reaches the city by bicycle or on top of someone's head. In fact, the cycle is pretty complete with that cow devouring an old string of blossoms [FIG. 45]. I guess the clatter, the downright mayhem of the city, is pretty evident here, too. There's an important, perhaps I should say critical, shot here in a typical narrow street where a funeral procession is on its way to Manikarnika [FIG. 46]. I think this is the first time that I shot this scene, and there is evidence for that in the fact that it is all happening some distance from the camera. I was still reticent about inserting myself in the midst of these processions. But maybe this is what makes this scene work. I don't really want people to know what they are looking at. I only want them to wonder what it might be; viewers should begin to deal with this in the same way required by the marigolds and the wood in this film. You could say that another piece of the puzzle is now available to fit into place.

FIG. 47

Then there is a cut here to an old lady, one of the familiar widows of Benares, don't you think, praying in Ragul Pandit's little shrine [FIG. 47]. This cut tries to put some further meaning into the preceding shot of the funeral procession by suggesting that there is something here to pray for or to be religious about. It's all part of the larger intention of describing Benares as a place that has so much to do with worship. This interlude in the shrine represents another, and very appealing, approach to the unknown.

AÖ There's a bird that flies into the scene.

RG Yes, and that's terribly important to me. I wish I could have been smarter about that bird. I saw it come and tried to do something with it, but it was too frightened and got away before I could do much of anything. It was a little like the Holy Spirit, at least in its evanescence. In the film, the lowly sparrow, which is what I think this is, comes back frequently to the Dom Raja, both in his house and at Manikarnika.

FIG. 48

AÖ In this shot of the lady outside the temple [FIG. 48], you can still hear Ragulji's recitation. She turns on her own axis: so characteristic! Such worship is seldom congregational in nature. On the contrary, it is very individual-istic and personal. What she's doing is so evocative of Eliot's "still center of the turning world." In Indian terms she is really circumambulating herself, her own divinity. You don't have to go to a place of pilgrimage. All this communicates easily to me; but I'm not sure whether that's because I associate it with Indian religious notions or because it is there in the image. However, when you see somebody doing this kind of thing, even if it's outrageously alien to you, you've got to be impressed with it, that self-absorbed movement . . . it is so obviously not silly.

RG There is some kind of curious, natural grace in it. I was thinking both when shooting and editing this that she was really a bird that had alighted here on this terrace and was doing her supplications, just like the sparrow that came to the altar inside.

At this point a whole new sequence begins. It is also another large piece of the bigger puzzle and is in the form of another simple but charged element, bamboo.

AÖ   I remember this well: how Om Prakash, as soon as he heard what was wanted, could translate the need into a real location. So it took no time at all to find this carpenter; except I also remember we went the first time only to find that he had gone to the hospital to see a relative.

RG   For all of its plainness, this bamboo takes on quite a lot of meaning. It gets very rich the further it is explored as an entity, common as it may seem at first. I remember many moments of impatience in Benares, and this could easily have been one of them, because I think we came back more than once trying to find the carpenter. When we did find him, I remember wondering what to do, thinking this is only bamboo, for God's sake, what can I make out of this? I suspect this is a question that comes up frequently in nonfiction work, and it's important to find the right answer. I'm not at all sure I did that here, but I remember trying. Actually, the way it was shot and the way it is used in the film do seem to offer some possibilities for a cinema that goes beyond mere observation.

FIG. 49

AÖ   In fact, it is something other than observation, which is a very literal kind of viewing of the world. It is an activity charged with the possibility of interpretation.

RG   Yes, since people and culture are not at all like ants and anthills, knowing about them is not as easy as just sitting down and watching them. There is the whole thing of people making meaning whenever they are doing something, even when they are chopping bamboo into pieces [FIG. 49] that are later tied together to make a ladder or a litter, or is it both? Isn't that really what we're suggesting is the problem for film?

AÖ   Yes, whether this bamboo worker does this mindlessly or whether his thoughts are on something else is quite immaterial; what is visually significant is that the grace and the style of his work are not mindless. The empiricists' way of deflating such statements as you've just made is to say, "Well, he was really only thinking about his breakfast or his nephew who is in the hospital

and not about the symbolic significance of what he is doing."
It may be true of that particular moment . . .

RG   Or even that particular man.

ÁÖ   . . . or that particular man. But the action and the position of
that action in the culture exist for everyone else; there is an
association with the other things you have mentioned and that are
suggested by the film. Passersby seeing this bamboo being worked
can, beyond just seeing something that is leaning against a wall,
easily reflect for a moment: this is the way we all go, this is the
way I'll be taken to the burning ground. So, too, with all ritual;
regardless of any individual's thoughts or
intentions, one can perceive in the performance its potential for the whole culture, for
the whole of humanity, because it's there in
the performance. Not only has this man
developed these motions over a span of thirty
or more years, but others have preceded
him for hundreds of years and in doing this
have guaranteed that the meaning is there
in the performance.

FIG. 50

**RG   The end of this bamboo sequence is a
rather studied and deliberate piece of
editing. I'm speaking now of the man who,
after he has made the ladder, squats down
to have a cigarette. The last shot of that
passage is of him exhaling [FIG. 50]. Here the
sound was enhanced to underline this letting
out of the breath. The shot is, of course,
referring to expiration—maybe all too
crudely, but I hope not. The other shot at the
end of this sequence is of a man who is
sleeping on a pile of unworked bamboo
poles [FIG. 51]. I can remember seeing that
scene the first time I went to this place, and
I knew that I should shoot it before he moved
or woke up because as an image it felt very
rich. So here it is connecting the bamboo**

FIG. 51

**sequence with the Mukti Bhavan Hospice sequence and giving a
distinct tone to the film at this point. Is it just a man sleeping
on some bamboo poles? Seen in its present context, it can't be
just a man sleeping on bamboo. Yet that was all he was doing.**

ÁÖ   Yes, he was just resting.

RG   And it's more than that, especially since it has been used to connect these two sequences of film.

AÖ   I also remember some corpses being carried past the bamboo working place.

RG   And we waited for them with the thought they might be something to film.

AÖ   . . . waited and talked about what it would mean to film such a procession from the point of view of the ladder maker.

RG   Nobody would have believed it was really happening.

AÖ   I remember distinctly that was what you said at the time: it would seem so obviously staged, even though it was absolutely authentic.

RG   Yes, I'm afraid that to have burdened this simple activity with all the meaning we have talked about and then to shoot a funeral cortege marching by in front of it would come off as something unquestionably contrived.

AÖ   Well, that's important. I mean, what doesn't end up in the film is as important in some ways as what does. It is symptomatic of the power to make things happen or make them not happen, and that says a lot about the very artificial crafting of these so-called real or actuality films. What is it that makes the "realness" of one scene more or less acceptable than some other scene? That would have been an entirely authentic procession going past a bamboo place, but there are different kinds of reality and they all take on a different significance.

RG   I think part of the problem is that the very act of filming changes the state of realness in things.

AÖ   Yes, yes.

RG   So making images in this ladder factory has changed things. I've begun to make it a little other than real by just being there and filming it.
      Here is the street outside the Mukti Bhavan. I guess we can both agree that this material is as important to the film as almost any other. Yet it was something I hesitated doing for quite a while. My first thought was that the film should not get as close

FIG. 52

FIG. 53

FIG. 54

to death as the Mukti Bhavan required. My intention was to keep things more remote, and so I felt I should avoid all head-on encounters with anything as potentially fatiguing as naked dying.

The opening shot of this sequence is of a cow and a prowling dog [FIG. 52]. The dog here is doing what it is meant to be doing, literally standing at the gateway between life, or the streets, and death, or the Mukti Bhavan. The other key shot in this first sequence about the Mukti Bhavan is the washing of the courtyard floor [FIG. 53]. There is much washing in this film, as one might expect. I suppose the Ganges flowing through the city is the governing image in this respect, but there is continuous reference to cleansing and purifying. Here the floor of the charnel house is washed of its recent death pollution and readied for its next. This is what I hoped would seep through to an audience.

AÖ   Yes, and then going up to that dazzling light [FIG. 54]. This sequence with the water and the light off the water is almost a purely visual element beyond the structure of the film. But when the camera tilts upward, it creates an opposition between above and below, light and darkness, and life and death. And this is very appropriate here since the experience of light, a dazzling brightness, is associated with death or transition to life after death. In any case, the imagery is of a piece with the sacred tradition. It's a little unearthly.

RG   I cannot help noting, somewhat ruefully, that the light that gets through to the nonfiction screen is often contingent on things well beyond the filmmaker's control. When it comes to getting the effect desired, intention very often gives way to accident. It is so different from narrative work, where one can control the light far more readily. However, in both cases—fiction and nonfiction—what the student of film sees decades or even just months after a film has been made is most likely a far cry from what anyone involved in its creation wanted seen. The reason is, of course, that as time goes by what is seen are copies, which are frequently many generations away from the camera negative and often badly marred from successive screenings. Among other problems this situation creates is one that our critical brothers and sisters ought to ponder, that of the infidelity of the evidence they so often use to support their complex theories about a film's meaning.

AÖ   The next question is whether, by accident or intention, the value of the kind we are talking about is actually achieving some kind of undeniable status. The light is there and is meaningfully relevant. How is this to be regarded? Should it be denied any significance because its tonal values were achieved accidentally? I keep wondering about this when I look at nonfiction film—particularly this one, where it seems to me the light is of a very special and varied kind that is beyond intention. In the prologue, for example, there are shots of heavy mist in the diffuse light that are followed in sequence by dogs fighting on the shore in a much brighter, clearer light. The juxtaposition of these shots is jarring. On the other hand, despite differences in tonal value, these images work well together.

　　Several things have come together while we have been talking: the chanting of God's name, the sound of the gong, and the ascent on the stairs to the dying women. The light that comes through the window at the top of those stairs is there whether you wanted it or not; it is an instance of the world of reality intruding despite all else. The light is beyond intention, and it has a very strong effect upon what we see.

RG   In fact, one of the few welcome accomplices of a nonfiction filmmaker is accident. There isn't much else helping us make these films. Actually, there is a whole lot conspiring against us. I really think that putting oneself in the position to encounter accident is very much a part of succeeding in this genre.

AÖ   I suppose that panning up to the light is no accident but really one of the tools of the trade. It's even one way of ending a sequence, right?

RG   It's a pictorial gesture, a choice made to provide another dimension to a shot which, as a result, might be useful in the editing process later on. The pan or tilt up you mention here was done with a certain desperation, as I remember; but then when

I saw it in the rushes there was this accidental capture of some very nice light. Anytime you see a tilt up from a scene, you can be pretty sure the camera operator has run short of better ideas. Nearly all the shots in this first Mukti Bhavan sequence were made with a view to what could be done with them in the editing. But without sitting at an editing table and discussing each one, it would be hard to explain the reasons behind all the choices made to get the shots that are actually included in the sequence as we see it here. Nevertheless, it's certainly possible to say they were framed far more with a view to editing than documentation.

AÖ   You and I know that we are in the Mukti Bhavan, and we know what takes place here; but as far as the viewer is concerned, what's behind this facade is a complete mystery. Still, the elements are very suggestive. For want of a better word, the opposition, or contrast, of going from water to light or sky to going, then, to the stairs has some communicative urgency, because these are elements that people already have seen and are familiar with.

FIG. 55

RG   Yes, these particular stairs [FIG. 55] fit in beautifully with the plan to use stairs as an indicator of transitions. I suppose this is an instance when I should be thankful for whatever accident put them into a house for the dying. Clearly, they were going to be the way the living reached the second floor and the way the dead were brought to the ground floor. I definitely thought about this as I was shooting. In the end, I think this seeking out of the meaning of things can have a large effect on the way the images look.

AÖ   In the shot of the procession of chanting attendants going up the stairs, the last person goes out of the frame and all you see are the stairs. As I recall, later in the film the camera parallels this ceremonial climb, but in the other direction: it alone descends to the ground floor, again showing you only the stairs themselves. This is very effective, but it's difficult to establish just why it is effective.

RG   The question I would like answered is when or even whether, with all the intentionality in the world putting as much metaphorical spin on the images as I or anyone else can manage, the audience is ever going to know that they are being asked to look at the stairs in this movie in a way they haven't thought to look at such things before. I think they will be willing to admit to a certain bombardment of their senses, but the question remains whether and how much they are focusing on the idea of stairs having more than just architectural significance. The reason I'm asking this question today is because last night I was reading George Eliot's *Middlemarch*, which I hope you agree may be the best anthropology of Victorian England. Anyway, she has this wonderful line in there where she says, "For we all get our thoughts entangled in metaphors and act fatally on the strength of them." I do often feel entangled in my thoughts. Maybe Eliot has given me a reason why. I'll just hope that I don't act fatally on them.

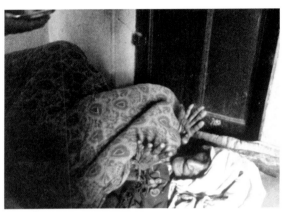

FIG. 56

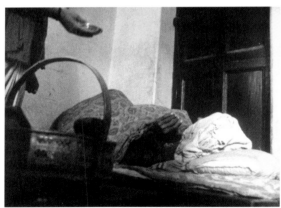

FIG. 57

AÖ Here is the first view of the old lady with her somewhat ambiguous hand movements [FIG. 56], which, if not entirely clear, certainly have a universality to them. There are also the small oil lamp, the bells, and the Ganges water poured into her mouth. All these have something to say to somebody from a Judeo-Christian tradition who's familiar with the last rites. It's very telling.

RG Yes, I was very moved by these ministrations and, though I'm fully aware I may be burdening the occasion with my own intentions and assumptions, I can't help feeling it is not being misread. There is the priestlike figure speaking scriptural words while trying to provide refreshment through this old lady's parched and motionless lips. This has to have some relevance outside the Hindu world. It is so clearly a rite of passage, don't you think?

AÖ At the very beginning of the sequence, when the ritualist picks up the tray, it is clear from the objects—flowers, water, and holy pictures—that it is some kind of solemn ceremony.

RG And a lamp [FIG. 57] and especially the gong that tolls and tolls.

AÓ Especially. Curiously enough, I heard some people say that they thought that when she was given the Ganges water, her hand gestures were an attempt to prevent the ritual from happening. It was read by them as rejection. That had never occurred to me.

RG **Indeed not, for me it was an eloquent "Yes, I'm still alive; I recognize that you're coming to me; I want you here; I want to taste Ganges water yet once again; I'm ready for this passage." That's what it said to me each time I saw it.**

AÓ That is what it says. She is just beginning to sail through that passage and is putting to use all the help available to her.

RG **But that is amazing. I never discussed that particular scene with anybody, but I wouldn't have thought for a moment that someone could come up with the idea that she is trying to ward off something. It seems so unmistakably welcoming as a gesture.**

AÓ It is not strange. You mentioned earlier your worry that people would not get the meaning that you tried to attach to images, and here is a case where at least some people have misread an image. I don't think this happens too often, but it would be interesting to find out when and why it does. The interchange here, during the repetition of God's name when the person being administered to assents in some way, is also mutual.

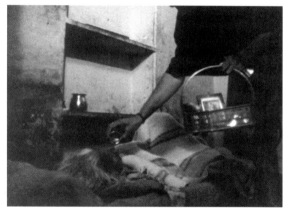

FIG. 58

RG **Yes, it seems so much like a last rite. This may be even clearer in the shot of the second lady** [FIG. 58].

AÓ Again, the dignity of all these figures—not just the dying inmates but everyone around them—is maintained.

RG **Yes, earlier we talked about the issue of dignity and how it's either preserved or denied and whether there might be something in the way the grammar of film is used that accounts for one or the other of these two end results. I sense it is likely that by taking pictures in certain ways you can be virtually certain to deprive people of their dignity. On the other hand, I can also see the possibility of an image style that will preserve or possibly enhance dignity. I suppose there might even be a problem here of overdignifying. But that seems to me more a special case of a general tendency to trivialize.**

FIG. 59

FIG. 60

FIG. 61

I should point out that in this next scene, where the ritualists are finished and going back downstairs [FIG. 59], we are getting a foretaste of an important later sequence in which the cadaver is brought down to the courtyard. Again, the important element in this shot from the balcony is the wet, newly washed floor of the courtyard [FIG. 60]. It is very deliberately framed, this washing. Then here is the cut to the "far shore" and the dog gnawing at some suspicious piece of dead meat [FIG. 61]. It could be the backbone of a mule, or it could be the thighbone of a man; I don't know what it is. At the time I didn't think it was human, but it clearly is meat and it's clearly a carnivorous act on the part of the dog.

AÖ It could be anything, including human; the human association is not exempted and is an important part of the ambiguity here.

RG Precisely.

AÖ And yet, in a certain sense, it makes no difference what this picture of meat is, because it is just a part of the larger cycle that will return everything to the beginning.

RG The courtyard is the major image here, even though the one that people seem most struck by is the dog scavenging that piece of meat. All I wanted was for an audience to associate death with that wet floor.

AÖ Yes, I remember that you wanted to make something of that wet floor, returning time and time again, probably to shoot it in different conditions. But in the film it's not the first time that water is shown to be regenerative, purificatory. So it's a very powerful thing. Mithai Lal is also giving water to the Shiva lingam.

RG Yes, he waters the deities like flowers.

ÁÖ   And so does Ragul Pandit. He makes water offerings; so there is a lot of water being manipulated.

RG   **In fact, I like to think water plays an important role as the solution and the salvation of everything.**

ÁÖ   And so from the beginning there is the river, the use of the river, and the use of water, particularly as holy water poured on the lips of the dying. One can read a lot into these images.

RG   **Yes, considering all the different ways it is seen or alluded to, it is obvious that water has pretty extensive meaning.**

ÁÖ   I wonder how far one can go developing the kinds of associations we are suggesting.

RG   **Not very far at all. I don't think that anything of the kind we have been discussing ever gets surfaced by people watching films. We are being very precise about our associations. The average viewer won't be. He or she will just undergo, at best, some strong but quite inarticulate feelings.**

ÁÖ   And any associations that do surface will justifiably be limited by the range of one's experiences.

RG   **I agree. We seem to comprehend the world in ways that the world itself provides for its comprehension, and metaphor is one of the tools at hand.**

ÁÖ   Well here . . . this brief shot is very nice showing the city shore behind the dog—it's beautiful. It's a kind of glistening, luminous city [FIG. 62].

FIG. 62

RG   **You mean the second shot with the dog eating in the foreground and the city in the background? This was intended to indicate that the dog is on the "far shore."**

ÁÖ   It's a peculiar thing. It occurs to me now that the far shore is also, peculiarly enough, ambiguously situated with regard to the local scheme of things. It's the place where nobody lives, it's the flood plain, and it's all the other things we already mentioned. For you, it was also, metaphorically, a place people are trying to reach to achieve salvation, to escape rebirth. It was also the place where, at a certain point, we wanted to film bhang chara, the preparation and drinking of bhang, something for which Benares is famous. Such things are a reminder of the joyful aspects of life, Benares as the city of good life.

RG   **But we never had the time, nor did I want any confusion about the meaning I was assigning that shore.**

AÖ   Still, it is also a farther shore in a joyful sense. I like the fact that it's not a shore explicitly or unequivocally filled with dread.

RG   **On the contrary: as you say, people went there on picnics that included some mind altering.**

AÖ   Which is again a ritual act.

RG   **I also recall men going there to wash their dhotis and do some mild calisthenics. It was not an entirely dreadful place by any means. But I have avoided a recreational tone as far as that shore is concerned, except for the boy flying a kite.**

FIG. 63

AÖ   And then these work shots. The sand-boats [FIG. 63] are very, very interesting, but, again, I'm not quite sure why they are there.

RG   **Here is a part of what I saw in Benares that truly fascinated me: this very simple, repetitive task. It's as elementary as anything that I'd ever seen human beings do, and it was something that I began to equate more with ant than human life. I was fascinated with the sight of these men and women going to the far shore to fill up an empty boat, then come back across the river and empty that boat of its sand on the near shore. There was what seemed to be a prodigious purposeless-ness to it. At the same time, it was in some ways almost Egyptian as spectacle. I remember first thinking, when working on this material, that this scene would stand for the great dreariness of so much that we know as human labor. What I've heard several times from some viewers is that they think these boats are carrying the ashes from the cremations. Of course, from a realistic standpoint, that's absolutely loony, and it astonished me when I first heard it. But in another way, sand is a kind of ashes. I mean, that notion fits with what I had in mind using the image,** because sand, for me, has always been an indicator of time. Think of the hourglass. We are all only so many grains of sand that have to get through the neck of something in order to register a lifetime. And then, as you may remember, there are two scenes where, after trying very hard, I managed to get sand spilling off this boat into the river. I suspect these are the images that call up the idea of ashes. They certainly were intended to say something about both mortality and the cyclical nature of existence. But we should get on with the film here.

It is now at some kind of midpoint, at least in running time.

FIG. 64

It is also midday in the temporal structure of things. What's to be seen here is the rowing down river of a boat carrying a corpse to Manikarnika [FIG. 64]. The boat is filled with relatives of the deceased. They are singing religious songs to a rather lively accompaniment. The mood is not at all joyless. I hoped to suggest something here rather than reveal it in detail. I wanted the audience, at this midpoint in the film, to wonder what was happening in this boat rather than know for a certainty that it was a dead man being carried down the river.

AÖ   Since there is no funeral procession chanting "Ram nam satya he," it has to be some sectarian variant. There is a reasonable question here, even for us, of what is going on.

RG   It's intended to act as a note, really, in the larger melody of what the river means and what it provides.

AÖ   So the continuity includes the sand workers, then the boat at a distance gliding, followed by a closer shot of the boat with the singing and music.

RG   There has been singing before in connection with a funeral procession, in the gully above Manikarnika. This idea of music and even dance on the occasion of death has been established.

AÖ   Some caste groups celebrate in the funeral procession with singing and dancing.

RG   There may be a filmmaker comment to make here about this seemingly very ordinary scene of a steep stairway following the corpse-in-the-boat shot. The stairway shot shows an old and blind man feeling his way down to the river with a very stout pole

FIG. 65

[FIG. 65]. In order to know where to put his foot, he finds the edge of the step by knocking at it with his pole. Ned Johnston, who was doing sound, had to be well out of the way because I was framing the shot very wide. So the recording was not what it should be. In the post-production process we had to make new sound for the whole sequence. The filmmaker comment is as follows: to make the shot of the old man work, something had to be invented, namely, some new sound. An old man who is blind is finding his way down the stairway, and that's all I wanted people to know; but they never would have known it with the original, muffled, hardly audible sync-sound track.

AÖ   The old man can be heard asking something about a ritual, whether it has started or not, but it would have been pointless to draw attention to this dialogue because it's one of those incidental things. I mean, on the way down the stairs to some other errand, he happens to meet someone.

FIG. 66

RG   The next cut is to something else coming down some other stairs—dead animals, in fact [FIG. 66]. Again, the sound of their descent was enhanced in order to define this particular space and in order to let people know that these are very hard stairs. The sound is as much a reality as the sight, and although the image of the head banging its way down the stairs is pretty graphic, it becomes much more graphic with the heightened sound underlining the whole thing.

It's clear from the sync track that the people passing each other on the steps are saying things to each other, but nobody has said that what they were saying was of such grave importance it should be translated.

AÖ   These scenes also show one of the more repulsive aspects of the mess in Benares.

RG   Definitely.

AÖ   Look at this pile of garbage being swept into the shape of some kind of animal's head

FIG. 67

[FIG. 67]. I'm surprised to be seeing pattern even in a random heap.

All this works in terms of the idea of the river as caretaker of life and death. Then the legitimate question comes up: at what point does the mess clog the river and defeat its purpose of regeneration and purification? I guess cultures are not very good at dealing with these kinds of questions, because practices and beliefs accumulate, and they all make perfect sense in the case of each animal being returned to the river or each corpse being immersed in it; but at some point, it becomes just too much for the river to handle, and then it becomes a matter of pollution rather than holiness.

RG   **Well, maybe the culture will invent better ways to handle this pollution.**

ÁÖ   This brings up a current problem. In interpreting situations like these, one has to walk the tightrope of discrediting what is going on while, at the same time, not ignoring it or engaging in apologetics. The images are not too overwhelming as evidence of the decay and corruption, which are also graphically there. But this is one of the interesting things about actuality film. It would have been very easy to show just that particular side: the depravity or the degeneracy of it all. But the other, meaningful side of the river as Goddess, as the Mother taking all her children into her lap, is also there. And, in a way, these shots of the animals being dragged down the stairs are just perfectly ordinary, an employee-like sweeper's act.

RG   **Completely.**

ÁÖ   Equally well, you can imagine a municipal truck picking up these carcasses and dumping them in some hole at the back of the city. That they end up at the edge of the river is another comment on the ambivalence of the sacred/nonsacred in Benares and how tradition can be used as an excuse for avoiding civic responsibility or whatever.

This sequence is very charged, because it points in so many directions. It certainly bears out what you intended with the steps. It also highlights the issue of transition for Benares. Obviously things are changing, and there is great difficulty coping. Things are falling apart and yet people are sweeping the stairs and trying to patch things up. The images here seem to me very dialectical and thoughtful. Beyond the merely abstract notion of metaphysical stairs and a farther shore, these images also illuminate the current situation.

RG   Yes, I know it is very much the here and now of Benares. But that was not what most interested me at the time, nor does it today. You are speaking of large social issues, and these must be dealt with; but my feeling is that the metaphysical stairs will always be there, even if dead donkeys are disposed of in the electric crematoria they were talking about getting.

ÁÓ   Stairs, carcasses, and refuse are multivocal symbols, and for that very reason they are elements of a local situation that is being politicized and is changing before our eyes.

FIG. 68

FIG. 69

RG   Here the film comes back to two important motifs: the marigold and the kite. The first is best seen developed in the image of the cow devouring the garland of marigolds [FIG. 68]. Even though it is a common thing to see in Benares, I can remember having some difficulty finding a cow doing that. I can even remember carrying my old garlands with me to feed the cows so that I would be sure to get my shot. Getting my camera out of its black plastic garbage bag in time to catch a cow scarfing down a garland was not the easiest thing to do either quickly or gracefully.

Perhaps next to the garland motif in importance is that of the kite. There were not as many kite-image possibilities as marigold ones. In this next shot is a little shop where a boy has come to buy a kite [FIG. 69]. It is in here to focus attention on kites in a context other than that of flight. It works a little like the earlier Mithai Lal shot in which, as I pointed out, he nearly steps on a kite as he's walking home from his bath. I remember once seeing a particularly hungry cow eating a fallen kite. I also remember taking some kites with me and trying, in vain, to find a hungry-enough cow. I thought that if I could get that image I would be making real progress toward developing the notion of organic circularity. I might also mention here that both the marigolds and the kites were, for me, very positive, and redemptive, as imagery.

There are a few almost informational shots here of the gullies and what goes on in them. Here, too, is a shot of one of the tiger sculptures on top of the wall at the Dom Raja's house.

I used this image several times to suggest both the owner and his line of work. The tigers or the birds of prey flying in circles above them were supposed to put a person in mind of that man and also of his role as a watchman on the banks of the river to the beyond. There are some more gully shots, including, again, a somewhat fragmentary and distant view of a funeral procession. On the track is the sound with which the audience will become very familiar: "Ram nam satya he." This is what I want to have stick in people's minds at this point.

AÖ   This passing bull makes me wonder why we did not make more of these holy animals.

RG   Because they had such different claims on people's attention?

AÖ   Also because they are so prevalent. It is strange I didn't think of this before. Maybe sacred cattle are so much a part of life in Benares that they are not conspicuous. But I don't remember having discussed with you whether they should be a part of the film.

RG   I suspect that people used to think that it was really very strange to see cows in the streets, but by now the general public has gotten so sophisticated about foreign countries, including "exotic" India, that they are no longer impressed by holy cows wandering about.

AÖ   Of course, bulls are a part of Shiva's entourage, just as dogs are. The association is there; however, you establish the link with the dogs, not with the cattle. Furthermore, in the film the dogs evoke Benares as well as Roman mythological associations.

The next scene is at the crossroads of the two main gullies that lead down to Manikarnika. What we hear is a devotional song

sung by a leper who is being pushed in a cart by his colleague in beggary [FIG. 70]. This particular man seemed to appear all over the city—in front of various temples and other prominent places. He wasn't so much a representative of the beggar population of Benares as he was an individual, a man with a fairly distinct personality whose whereabouts one could determine according to the time of day.

RG   I'm not sure what most interested me about this little pair, but I know that I was

FIG. 70

very taken by the song. I felt a great absence of music in Benares, a lack of musicality of any kind, and so when I heard this I knew that I would use it. There also was something wonderfully incongruous about the lilt and drive of this song that was coming out of such a dreadfully afflicted body. It was pure as music, especially in that there was no accompaniment, except for the clatter and creak of the singer's broken-down cart as he was pushed through the cobblestone gullies. The shot is there for its graphic and musical qualities. It is certainly cinematic, at least in terms of nonfiction. Making the shot was not easy, I remember. As you can see, some children step in front of me at a certain point. I had to lift the camera up to see past them. I must say though, compared to most Indians of all ages, they were remarkably oblivious of the camera.

FIG. 71

The cut is to a shot of a very pathetic dog that "lifts its leg" on some garbage piled into a corner of the stairway [FIG. 71]. The shot is put here to accent what came before it. The leper and the dog are two denizens of the same precincts, and, as God's creatures, they share, to a certain extent, similar destinies. The steps, which come in again here, are also accented or inflected by this dog doing what it's doing. Maybe it all says something about how the way to the next life is strewn with more than flowers.

AÖ   Yes, I remember we talked about this, and I can see what you're trying to do. I don't have a very strong opinion one way or the other about this particular shot. If it were longer (and it may have been at some point during the editing), it would have just drawn attention to itself. As a short reminder that functions almost like a sign rather than a symbol, I see the sense in it. But, for me, it doesn't especially reinforce the idea of the circularity of things decaying. All of this is so clear from other parts of the film that here it is not really necessary. The idea would come across if the shot weren't there. It's not graphic enough. It's a messy business because the shot emphasizes the dirt rather than the stairs. It's not very clear, and that painful dog—yes, I feel ambivalent about it.

RG   Right. Now it passes from that stairway, the dog and stairway shot, to the wood-selling place above Manikarnika Ghat. This sequence is important because it is here that the already

FIG. 72

FIG. 73

much-heard sound of wood being split is first comprehended. Woodworkers are busy splitting some of the enormous trunks of trees that have been brought by barge [FIG. 72]. Here, also, one understands the meaning of another small mystery, which is the scale that weighs the wood to be used in the cremation fires [FIG. 73]. The scale was first seen, I believe, when Mithai Lal was going down to his bath in that very early sequence. It has also been acting as a kind of question mark in several other scenes. What is this? What does this thing do?

ÁÖ This is a very important sequence, I think.

RG Yes, it begins to clarify some things that up until now have been relatively ambiguous, such as the scenes of the corpses being carried on litters. After this it will be pretty hard to escape the fact that these are dead bodies that are being taken somewhere. The connection between the bamboo worker and these litters hasn't been made, but it's about to be.

ÁÖ This sequence is very rich because it brings together these short shots of the stairs, the sound of the wood being split, the woodpiles, the scales, the dogs, the boats, and the river; so they are incredibly charged.

RG Maybe also incredibly layered. I mean this in at least two ways. Images can be layered in a largely optical sense with many things happening in the frame, even on various planes within the frame. In addition, an image can be layered as to the significance or meaning of its content. In this case, the optical layering can be minimal since what is in question is what the image is signifying. In the case of the sequence we have been looking at, I think that the image is both very active optically and very rich symbolically. There is the interesting question still of how things get into an image, how the world is interrogated and then apprehended by a camera. What we are looking at here seems to me to be very much the world the way it is—but strained or, better, filtered through the sensibilities of the

FIG. 74

FIG. 75

operator/observer. So it can be, though it doesn't have to be, a very shaped vision. Nevertheless, the vision is grounded in the world as it is. To the extent that what one sees is the world as it is, one is also being presented with certain inescapable and widely shared meanings. To the extent that what one sees is a highly shaped vision of that same world, one is being offered more private meanings.

AÖ It may not be clear to the viewer that it is a human-being's worth of wood being measured here [FIG. 74] and that what immediately follows is a funeral procession [FIG. 75]. However, the link between the shots is pretty explicit.

RG For all anyone knows, that wood is for the body that's going by; I mean, it most likely isn't, but, as you said, in the editing the two are connected.

AÖ So a lot of things are coming together for the first time.

RG And we're getting physically closer and closer to these litters until, finally, we will see the litter for what it is, a ladder made of bamboo.

AÖ This is almost a quotation of the shot of the river bank.

RG Exactly. This is an echo of that earlier sequence of bringing wood down to the river to be rowed up to Manikarnika.

AÖ Yes, with the empty scale and the boats this becomes a central assemblage of probably not more than a few seconds.

RG Well, maybe less than a minute, depending on where you start timing.

AÖ From the beginning of the wood splitting . . .
This next sequence draws a lot of themes together, and then ends up with another question by returning to a shot negating closure: the balance freely swinging in the air [FIG. 76].

FIG. 76

FIG. 77

RG Empty. Waiting for the next dead person.

ÁÖ Yes, nothing is resolved. This is the cycle.

RG Yes, the scales will keep on swinging.

ÁÖ You return at this point to the wood barge with its creaking oars [FIG. 77]. This hasn't been seen for some time.

RG No, but the editing implies that the boatman has been rowing ever since we first saw it push off from Raj Ghat, where the wood was loaded. This inference, hopefully, is also supported by the film's temporal structure, which encompasses the action within a period between two consecutive sunrises. Since the boatman started rowing at about 9:00 A.M. and he is about halfway through a four-hour journey up to Manikarnika Ghat, real elapsed time may be more like a couple of hours.

ÁÖ The shot of the washermen on the bank, it seems to me, is an example of a fairly rare concern with ordinary activity.

RG A quasi-historical footnote regarding this short passage may be appropriate at this point. I'm sure you can hear in the shots of the washermen the braying of a donkey. The other dominant sound is the creaking oarlocks. Perhaps you remember that there is a donkey braying loudly at the beginning of *Rivers of Sand*. Both instances are gestures to Luis Buñuel, who created one of cinema's most powerful nonfiction scenes using a donkey that has been bitten to death by bees. This was in *Land Without Bread*. He also put a memorable donkey into *Un chien andalou*.

ÁÖ Yes, I remember.

RG Now here are some more echoes, Ákos. I suspect you are by now fully aware of the purification theme. It is amplified here with a scene of a woman cleaning the Dom Raja's courtyard [FIG. 78], which is a little like Hercules trying to clean up the Augean

FIG. 78

stables. **Of course, it is also an echo of the courtyard being washed at the Mukti Bhavan.**

AÖ   The stacks of bamboo poles against the walls are significant for us, but I'm not sure the association is made by most viewers. There are so many that they look like a whole forest [FIG. 79].

FIG. 79

FIG. 80

RG **Yes, we know that these poles are some kind of tribute to the Dom Raja and that they come from the cremation ground after the litters have been taken apart following the lighting of the funeral pyres. I never did find out what happened to the poles after they were collected at the Dom Raja's.**

AÖ   I think he sells them.

RG **As for an audience getting everything there is to know about these bamboo poles, it would be ridiculous to suppose any such thing. On the other hand, I don't see how some recognition could be avoided. So many nearly identical objects leaning up against a house should arouse at least minimal curiosity.**

AÖ   This shot reminds me of a structurally similar scene: that of the beggar singing. As you mentioned a moment ago, we see the beggar from behind some children who are standing in the foreground. In this shot, you have framed three of the Dom Raja's attendants in the foreground [FIG. 80], and we see the Dom Raja through them, so to speak. Here you have not a beggar king but a real king. This sound track, as in the shot with the beggars, is extremely rich with animal and bird sounds. There is also the seemingly incoherent muttering of the king himself speaking to these reverential listeners.

RG **Perhaps more feudalistic than reverential . . .**

AÖ   Especially the man with the white hair, who acts like a courtier in the Privy Chamber beholding the king's preparations for the day. There is definitely a regal air to this. The beautifully washed floor and that incongruous briefcase add to it. It's a

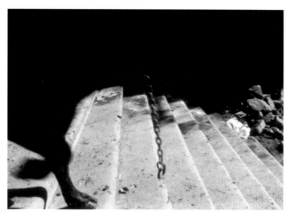

FIG. 81

FIG. 82

FIG. 83

wonderful scene that you can read many ways. You can read it structurally, with little trouble, and you can luxuriate in the richness of the filming, which brings up so many associations. These associations, incidentally, are not contradictory; they're layers rather than competing images.

RG So off the Dom Raja goes to his appointed round, which will undoubtedly take him to the burning ground.

The next cut is to a very large and somewhat sinister animal that seems almost to fall down a steep stairway above the ghats [FIG. 81]. I am using this for its graphic possibilities more than for any other reason. Maybe this enormous accumulation of fat and flesh (like the Dom Raja himself) can indicate the fullness of life as much as the darker side of the stairs down which it is headed. Later on, the buffalo comes back in the kite scenes as a somewhat troubling "familiar." I will want to say more about it when we get to that section of the film.

The next scene is of the Mukti Bhavan, where the ritual attendants are engaged in their vigil and are singing sacred songs. There is a shot of the washed courtyard suggesting, again, its readiness to receive a new corpse. Then we have one of the key shots of the whole bamboo story, a man carrying a small ladder through the gates of the hospice [FIG. 82]. It is still a ladder—but only until the next sequence, when all that changes. For all anyone knows up to this point, this is a person who is coming to wash the windows.

AÖ Then the ladder is just put against the wall [FIG. 83].

RG Yes, here is a very short shot of the ladder by itself against the wall. This shot is so selective in the narrowness of its angle that people watching have to ask themselves what it means, why they are being asked to look at this piece of third-world carpentry.

FIG. 84

FIG. 85

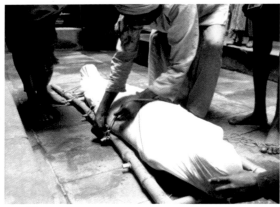

FIG. 86

Someone is trying to tell the audience that a bamboo ladder is more than a bamboo ladder. So we go from that to what we were talking about earlier, the camera floating, in the Mukti Bhavan, down the same stairwell [FIG. 84] that had previously been seen from below as the attendants went up to minister to their charges. Then we cut to a reverse shot of something being carried: the corpse being carried down the steps [FIG. 85]. And the connection is made, finally and unmistakably, between death, bamboo ladder, and courtyard. Here it all comes together for the first time—all these elements, including the marigolds, which will soon appear. I suppose this is when you might ask why it took so long—why all this ambiguity and mystery about these things I've called simple elements? I'm not sure, except that I thought that the audience would not simply wait for the mysteries to be dispelled but would come up with their own solutions, supply their own answers, and so, in that way, they would be doing their own anthropology. They would, in Cliff Geertz's words, be "finding their feet."

AÖ   As I look at this event, this death, I'm reminded of its specific nature; we happened to be there when it occurred, and so we were, in a sense, attendants at this woman's funeral service [FIG. 86]. But it could have been any other of the hundreds of deaths that occur in Benares every day. It was this one, and it was not at all sumptuous. In fact, it was a simple, almost destitute occasion; and yet the position of the event in the film does not rest on the poverty of the arrangements. It's a curious thing that being so simple was almost better than had it been ornate.

RG   I agree with you completely. It was elemental just the way a marigold is.

AÖ   I suppose it was what almost anybody could count on as a minimum in this society—at least this much attention to the fact that one has died. It was also the bare minimum provided by this particular charity, the Mukti Bhavan; but, even so, it was filled with dignity and some concern on the part of the participants.

RG   I think that the care and orderliness one sees in the way this event is handled is what confirms that dignity.

ÁÖ   So one is not really concerned here with a particular instance, a Hindu death ritual, as much as with a greater flow of things, with death itself. It has an almost medieval "Everyman" quality to it.

RG   Precisely. In fact, I was just going to say "everyman," except it's really "everywoman" in this case, and I'm really not sure how different the thing would look if this had not been one of our old ladies. But I am convinced that if it had been an elaborate sort of thing with high Brahminic undertakings and displays of wealth, much of the elemental meaning would have been buried in the debris of all those details.

ÁÖ   Yes, it says what we all know about having to deal with death alone, but it is also comforting to realize that people keep ministering, that it's not just a pile of garbage we leave behind. Certainly there is a loneliness to it, but even where there is hardly any family involved and things are as lonely as they can get, it is not that terrible. It may be a factor, but here, at least, I do not see what other people might regard as the poverty of the lower-class Indian way of death. Still, I'm struck by the contrast between this and other deaths I have seen in much richer communities in India.

RG   Where there is great pomp and ceremony, not just one pathetic garland [FIG. 87] but rickshaw loads of them?

ÁÖ   Yes, curiously enough, the death rituals of different classes differ mostly just in terms of embellishments. This, the simpler ceremony, is more telling because you see clearly how the elements come together.

RG   There is not very much to say about the editing of this sequence except that it is very straightforward. I'm really just following the action; everything is in its actual, real-world order. I do remember, while shooting this,

FIG. 87

worrying that the garland of marigolds was so inconspicuous it might not be seen.

AÖ What about that shot of the lone survivor, the woman at the edge of things, the woman in the shadows?

RG She is hardly visible, unfortunately. I don't think the shot works particularly well, but for some reason I felt compelled to leave it in. It is a case of my better cinematic sense being over-ruled by some scruple about content. I noticed this lady hovering in the shadows and then darting forward to put something on the litter as it was lifted up to be taken out of the courtyard. She was as furtive as the sparrows that came when the little funeral group had disappeared, except the birds got the few grains of rice or candy that had spilled off the litter. I never saw that person again, but I do remember her upstairs near the fires that cooked the little bit of food given the dying inmates. About all that can be said is that she was there and was a part of the human interaction taking place. It is hard to know sometimes when the requirements of continuity must overrule the need for thorough documentation. I think what I would say is that both

FIG. 88

are valid concerns but that, unless the cinematic criteria are met, it hardly matters how much is reported. If it is not seen well, it will probably achieve the equivalent of invisibility. This sequence is largely over by the time the body has left the courtyard and the sparrow has come to replace it. I wonder if there is any association in people's minds between this shot and the gyrating woman praying on Ragul Pandit's balcony while the bird pecked at his altar.

Finally, the body is carried out through the gates of the Mukti Bhavan and, with a newly washed courtyard floor [FIG. 88], the cycle is ready to start again. It all had a certain inevitability for me as I watched it happening. Nonetheless, as the sequence dealing explicitly with death at the Mukti Bhavan ends and the film moves on, so does this small package of humanity. Thus, the next shot is another view of the wood barge [FIG. 89], a more implicit allusion to the same subject.

The whole anthropology of Manikarnika

FIG. 89

Ghat has yet to be seen, and the wood barge moves us in that direction. Speaking of anthropology, there is, I would suppose, a fair amount stored away in nearly all the images we've seen.

ÁÖ Yes, there's no question the anthropology is there, and one certainly could make something of it by writing about it independently. You could also compare the images and the words in an attempt to see the relationship between them. I'm interested in the anthropology as a background from which these images emerged. I'm not sure who needs it, but there is also a philosophy embedded in the anthropology. Maybe that's what we are trying to get at in this discussion.

FIG. 90

FIG. 91

RG Anyway, we are getting closer to Manikarnika, closer to seeing the edge of that shore and what goes on there. There is a shot of a dog scratching fleas on the stairs at Manikarnika [FIG. 90] that I employed, circuitously, to open up the whole business of cremation. These brief scenes are then followed by a short sequence of which I am very fond. It is this one of the sand barge being poled up the river by that solitary voyager [FIG. 91]. The barge is laden with the sand that, earlier in the day, cinematically speaking, had been gathered up on the far shore and is now being taken to a place on the "living" side of the river. This small group of shots of the sand boat develops the theme, which was introduced in the prologue, of this curious industry. It is followed by a shot of another kind of boat, much smaller, that is carrying a rower, some passengers, and an ambiguous bundle on its fore deck [FIG. 92]. With good enough eyes it would be possible to see that the bundle is loosely tied to a flat rock. Nothing on the sound track gives any precise information as to what this craft's mission might be. But, here again, it is my assumption that the audience will correctly sense they are witnessing a burial in the river.

FIG. 92

FIG. 93

AÖ   Yes, and I also think that the experience is actually intensified by not having to directly witness the burial in close-ups.

RG   **It is hard to know when recognition begins. I assume that the shot of an oar dipping into the river to the accompaniment on the track of the creaking of our persistent oarlock plays a part in telling the viewer what is going on. Incidentally, in that scene of the oar you may never have noticed that near the top of the frame is the extremely spooky appearance and disappearance of one of those Ganges dolphins [FIG. 93]. They completely eluded all my intentional efforts to film them. I did not know I had actually recorded one on film until I came back and saw this shot in the rushes. This is another of those strangely magical nonfiction moments. Here, in this shot which comes right after a body has been consigned to the river, appears an almost fabulous denizen of the deep.**

AÖ   This passage of the boatman and the sand barge may stand for very different things. Coming after the Mukti Bhavan scene, it can be thought of as a continuation of a journey as well as a secular activity. Then, the creaking oar and the coming into view of the whole Manikarnika landscape carry so many possibilities. Not to mention that amazing porpoise, which creates even more possibilities. What is it doing there? Most people just don't believe such a thing could be in the river, this enormous animal. It creates an underwater presence, almost the antithesis of the water buffalo on the stairs. Then the boat finally arrives at its destination at Manikarnika, which up until now has been only glimpsed in a few scenes.

RG   **. . . such as where the dog is scratching his fleas.**

FIG. 94

AÖ   Yes, but now it's more extended. There were only indications of the place until now.

RG   **And now it is going to be revealed . . .**

AÖ   The platform, one of the burning platforms still steaming. Water again . . .

RG   **And the scale [FIG. 94].**

<u>AÖ</u>   . . . and then everything in context with the sound of wood being split and the wood barge actually docking. A strangely calm time at the ghat.

<u>RG</u>   Yes, it's hot, it's midday. But people sometimes must do essential work, and so it goes on.

We're two-thirds of the way into the film, where the wood boat which has been rowed up river from Raj Ghat has just made fast at Manikarnika Ghat. The following shot is of a water buffalo distractedly munching something at the river's edge. The wood barge is in the background.

FIG. 95

It's the next shot that is of interest as a piece of camera graphics, because it shows how the elements we have talked about so much in earlier sequences can be combined in a single image [FIG. 95]. It includes, prominently in the foreground, a wood scale and, on the parapet of a wall behind, a boy trying to launch a kite. This was a popular place to bring a kite, owing to the prevailing updrafts from the cremation fires. Then there is a shot, really a sequence of shots, that shows a small shrine near the burning ground itself. I wonder, again, how an audience that doesn't have any special knowledge of Benares is going to be aware of its history and ethnography the way we are. I happen to know this is an important shrine, but to look at it one might well wonder. It is like so many Indian sacred places in being rather dilapidated. I was drawn to this place by the sparrows that were pecking at some rice and other offerings. I don't know whether the audience sees these connections. I would be content if they merely registered the facts: fires, scales, boys, kites, thermals. I'm confident they would then, at some level of their imagination, work out their meaning.

FIG. 96

<u>AÖ</u>   The shot before that was of smoking ashes and embers and then, after the scale and kite, the lingam with the birds [FIG. 96].

<u>RG</u>   Yes, I remember thinking that the birds made an interesting comment on the proceedings that surrounded them.

FIG. 97

FIG. 98

The next scene is an example of the strategy I've already spoken about that takes the audience into a subject obliquely instead of headlong. I'm referring to the shot of the lady who is fishing for usable fuel in the embers of an old cremation [FIG. 97]. Making this kind of shot is a way of almost backing into a subject, since it says something about the end of a process rather than its beginning. On the other hand, it doesn't seem to me to matter where in a process you begin, if the logic you have adopted is that everything belongs to an endless cycle of events. So when you get up to this point where the wood has been weighed and is dropped on the ground [FIG. 98], what you have is another clue as to what is happening. The sound of the wood falling on the ground is meant to refer you back to the earlier wood splitting. If not, then at least these new sounds make one that much more intimate with wood as a substance. This wood business, you remember, started back in the main titles, where the track was carrying the sound of a tree falling in the forest. The intention is that, one by one, these clues will permit one not only to see but also to think about what's happening.

<u>AÖ</u>   Clearly, you can piece together what's happening from these different fragments. Actually, you could do this with one of the wide-angle shots that has most of the process happening somewhere in the frame. All you have to do is look hard and long enough at the right piece of film. Equally clearly, the idea here is not just to provide information.

<u>RG</u>   Manikarnika is truly a place of power. There is a real alpha-omega quality to it. At any point in time, everything is happening: beginnings, middles, and ends. At any one moment, all of life is revealed. It is virtually inexplicable chaos, which I chose to look at in terms of its details as well as its totality. When you go to Manikarnika for the first time, it's overwhelming—at least it was for me. I couldn't sort it out. I couldn't tell what the flow of time had to do with the progress of events I beheld because everything was so onrushing.

AÖ   Yes, even if you can't take it all in as a whole, its simultaneous diversity has a specific place in the Benares scheme of things, and there would be somebody who could make sense of these specifics. I mean, this could be done in terms of the traditional meaning of these things or from some other, perhaps semiological, perspective. There would be some way of making sense of each element.

The totality shown here in its confusion is, even for the people of Benares, broken down into separate streams, just as it is in the film. While there isn't anybody who can deal with all of Benares, one may note the separate aspects or layers. For example, one could make sense of the shot of the fires in terms of the people there, the temples, the Dom Raja, the beggars, and so forth. These distinct perspectives don't always belong in a single view of the world; so, in a way, they are multiple worlds, and not all of them hang together in a single, perfect structural whole. This, it seems to me, is what the film is addressing with close-ups and other devices. This is not to deny any specific vision or even abstract, overarching constructs. But some of the elements are just there, and they cannot be molded to fit some neat, preconceived structure. Some even contradict each other.

RG   I might say that the effect of the place on me was sometimes numbing in its capacity to bewilder. Often I really couldn't make out what was going on. What guided me photographically, however, was a feeling that a sure way to lose an audience was to stick their noses in naked death. I think I learned that lesson, if I didn't know it already, from my work in New Guinea. I also think that someone watching the grand confusion of Manikarnika through a wide-angle lens is no more likely to do any better than I did with my naked eyes. Hence I take "refuge" in marigolds, kites, wood, or bamboo. In these real objects, the mind, in Johnson's words, "can repose on the stability of truth," even if they are small truths. It can also hide from the bombardment of complex and sometimes startling behavior. If one is watching something that elicits no more than, "Oh, there's a kite flying above the heat of the fires," it means the mind probably is both relaxed and open. The next possibility is that someone would start building, out of what he or she sees, a little symbolic meaning: that the kites speak of life, play, and the more redemptive side of things, for example. I don't think such ideas would be possible if the images were reporting strictly observationally on the business of burning bodies.

We have gotten now to a place in the film where I made a particularly difficult editorial decision. It concerns the boat that was being repaired next to the cremation ground. You remember,

FIG. 99

I'm sure, my plan early on to work with this boat [FIG. 99]. I thought I could use it as a small narrative that might help give some structure to the film. I also thought that, being so close to the burning ground, it might give me a chance to have another, oblique view of what was, at the beginning, a most mysterious and problematic place. We did not know that we would eventually be allowed to do whatever we wanted at Manikarnika. It's interesting that this boat, initially approached with such enthusiasm, ended up occupying a relatively minor position in the film.

AÖ   This is an interesting issue. The material on the rebuilding of the boat could have become something like the story of the marigolds. I mean, it's complete enough to have a larger role. Now it exists mainly as outtakes.

RG   Well, it is pretty complete. But what does that mean? The reason it didn't find a more prominent place in the film is that when the structural idea of a film existing between two sunrises took over, material concerned with the rebuilding of a boat over a ten-week period was no longer very appropriate. I suppose if it were irresistible as film, a way could be found to put it into any structure. In fact, that would have been an interesting problem in editing.

AÖ   I can see it as a flashback during the launching. Can you remember any such thing in nonfiction film?

RG   Oh yes. In *The Hunters,* if you remember, the principal figures' individual characters and idiosyncrasies are developed with material drawn from different times of their lives. I think historic footage, which is really what we are talking about in that case, often has tremendous conviction to it. After a certain number of years, nonfiction film acquires more and more the status of document, and when it is used to give evidence or witness it seems to carry an undeniable authority. I'm not sure this is always deserved. It may arise from the fact that things that are old speak to us with a wisdom attributable largely to age.
The use of boat material in this film is really pretty straightforward. Beside its "ethnographic-ness," it may also offer some interest in the way it parallels the funeral occurring

FIG. 100

FIG. 101

simultaneously a few dozen yards down river. The editing here is both very deliberate and very coincidental. By this I mean that it was my intention to make a comparison by intercutting the launching of a "newborn" boat [FIG. 100] with the offering to the Ganges of a "newdead" person [FIG. 101]. It is highly coincidental that at exactly the moment the boat was taken down the steps to the river, a very sumptuously decorated body was on its way to being immersed. Here is a good case of actuality outdoing artifice. Nevertheless, despite this sanction of reality, the inference might be drawn that the actuality is too contrived. I have not felt it was a mistake to use this comparison, only that it failed to be entirely convincing.

AÖ   Yes, there is no question now that the boat is very close to Manikarnika.

RG   No question for us, because we have in our heads the exact geography of where the boat was.

AÖ   Well, at the end of the sequence the question is answered.

RG   I hope that it is, but in nonfiction you can't be sure. You are always at the mercy of a reality to which you constantly adapt but cannot arrange to suit your purposes. That's what I tried to do here. But, as I said, I'm not convinced it was successful. Reality may just have been too intractable.

AÖ   There is some smoke, that should help. And there are other indications.

RG   You may have noticed that the ritual at the "rebirth" of the boat is pretty complete. For example, when those hands are printed with yellow ochre on the pavement [FIG. 102], I actually show all five times it happens. It would have been very easy to begin the shot with the third or fourth time it's done. It's a little like the three blowings of the conch at the beginning of the film. I think that five is an auspicious number on an occasion like this, so, ethnographically speaking, there may be a reason for

FIG. 102

shooting and editing the scene to include it all. Also, when the red dot is made on the yellow hands five times, I shot each one of those actions, too. There is also the point that this ritual's rhythm is being determined by things like five hand prints, then five red dots, one circumambulation, etc. Nonfiction films, especially those made for commercial release, will not usually give more consideration to the original shape of the behavior than to the editorial requirements of keeping the film moving. But my feeling on this is that if you ignore the internal rhythms of things, you stand to lose more than just authenticity.

AÖ   Yes, it makes a difference in the way the film feels. It is obvious after a while when a film has been taken over by exclusively cinematic concerns. You can see what is important to the filmmaker.

RG   I seriously question, though, that anyone would feel differently about Mithai Lal if he blew his conch shell only once.

AÖ   Well, it's a question of authenticity: it could have been left at one, but that would have been a choice that would have signaled something either in terms of the filmmaker's intention or in relation to the integrity of the material. There is something satisfying in seeing somebody put all those red dots where they belong and having that little story unfold.

The relationship between boat and corpse is then further developed in a similar link between this next funeral pyre and the body that is placed upon it. The pyre is almost boat-shaped. And, as the corpse is lifted, we see a glimmer of the same shades of marigold that color the following scenes of the boat.

RG   What you're seeing is something very deliberate in the photography and in the editing of this whole little ritual about the boat. It's very complete. The shooting was thorough, and the editing retained proportionately much more than is usual of what actually happens in the real-time situation. In contrast, the shooting and the editing at Manikarnika was far more fragmentary and selective. The idea was to inform by indirection, if not outright withholding.

FIG. 103

FIG. 104

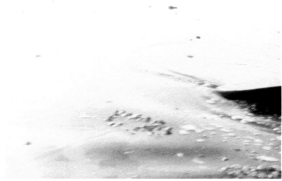

FIG. 105

ÁÖ   In this scene of the man pouring water over the bow of the boat [FIG. 103], the gesture is obviously the same as that of the relatives pouring water on the lips of the deceased [FIG. 104]. I suppose that by putting these shots together you are making some kind of comment on the sacredness of the Ganges and gestures of worship.

RG   At this point, you can probably see the problem with editing this way, or one of the many problems. The one that comes to mind is that when you edit the corpse and boat in this connective way, the audience may be led to assume there is something more than symbolic linkage: for example, that the corpse is going to go into the boat or that the boat once belonged to the corpse. But that may be part of the price you pay in order to get the effect you want.

ÁÖ   Eventually it becomes clear that they are separate and parallel.

RG   Yes, I think here where the body has been put in the water and the boat has been put in the water that the idea of two things being launched into the river is pretty clear. Just as a boat is put into the water to navigate a new geography, so a body is presented to the water for its imminent journeying.

ÁÖ   Then we go back to the water with marigolds floating on the surface [FIG. 105]. The boat just slips through them.

RG   You can see at this point, I guess, that what I'm trying to do in the editing is to move the meaning of the film from death in Benares to journeys to any far shore. Much of the imagery is very specific to this locale and has to do with what is happening in Benares; but some of it is not. The difficulty with film is that it is so literal and specific in the way it points to things. It's often hard to obscure with film, or even to generalize or achieve abstraction. It is so faithful in the way it reports the world. What I was hoping

to do here was to persuade the audience to think in terms of other histories, mythologies, and places.

This is also the place in the film where various motifs and other strands are brought together contextually so that an audience can see what they mean. Soon, for instance, you will see for the first time a funeral cortege in its totality and close up. It will no longer be particularly ambiguous. The film begins to pay off in terms of the audience's active, meaningful synthesis of the fragments and clues it has been given thus far.

FIG. 106

AÖ What I see are men carrying or dragging various burdens; then you cut to a group of men carrying a litter with a body. I think this is one of the few times you follow a procession from the point of view of the mourners. Now, at this point, you follow a blind man: another blind man, in the gully [FIG. 106]. I remember you said at the time that until he put his foot in a pile of cow dung, you had not been sure that he was blind. Anyway, he is a shrouded and mysterious figure.

RG You never see his face.

AÖ No, and it is difficult to infer from the way he gets around that he is blind.

RG Exactly. It's a good example of the blind leading whoever can or wants to follow. Life is pretty problematic, but we develop incredible strategies despite the most daunting handicaps. This is not the best of all possible worlds, as I've already quoted Buñuel. It has all kinds of problems and difficulties, and not the least of them is finding one's way. In fact, finding one's way perhaps best sums up the biggest dilemma of all: just getting there, wherever that may be. I remember when I shot this scene that what attracted me to it had nothing at all to do with what we are now discussing. It was what he was wearing. He had on the most beautifully laundered and pressed kurta I had ever seen in a city known for its clean clothes. It was the starkness of the contrast between his dress and the mess through which he was navigating so delicately that caught my eye. I finally realized by the way he was holding his left hand [FIG. 107] that he was

FIG. 107

MAKING FOREST OF BLISS

blind. His hand was like a magic wand or antenna that informed him and his surroundings of his coming and of the shape of the obstacles around him. I was amazed by this triumph over vicissitude.

ÁÖ Yes, the movement is really nice. The dog looks lost in comparison.

RG Now begins a stream of death going down toward Manikarnika.

ÁÖ Past marigolds [FIG. 108] . . .

FIG. 108

RG Yes, past marigolds and past life of all kinds, past tea stalls and little shops of notions and trinkets. It's death in the very midst of life and life in the very midst of death.

ÁÖ Then an amazing array of different corpses, some heavily and some lightly decorated.

RG I think our information was that somewhere around 150 bodies were burned at Manikarnika every day. I wonder if when an audience looks at this film they get a feeling for a number like this. That would be a lot of corpses to put into even a ninety-minute informational film. At this point, the shots of bodies coming down on litters to the burning ground are interrupted by a few cutaways, such as this one of a man squatting to urinate in a corner of the gully [FIG. 109]. I do not find this the least bit offensive, but I will concede that I may be in a minority. Then comes a shot of steps to keep this element, or motif, in the mind's eye. And then there is a scene of a little girl splitting some wood [FIG. 110]. The shot is in here to produce acoustic as well as visual echoes of the adult activity. It's a little bit depressing, perhaps, a little bit gloomy to think that whenever you stop to look at something in Benares you can be reminded of death.

FIG. 109

FIG. 110

FIG. III

FIG. II2

FIG. II3

AÖ This just happens to be, I think, the house of the Dom Raja's brother, with whom he shares the concession at Manikarnika.

RG Right, you can recognize this house by those frescoes on the exterior walls.

AÖ But here you have deliberately interjected what looks like a dead dog [FIG. III].

RG The dead dog is deliberate. At least, I thought the dog was dead. It may have been sound asleep, but I think it was dead. I don't think you can tell by looking at this image, and I don't think it makes any difference. The very ambiguity contributes nicely to the effect I wanted. In any case, it is the transition image to the Dom Raja.

AÖ In close-up. It interests me that the Dom Raja occupies basically the same light and space we saw at the Mukti Bhavan, where the light came from above and was very bright. He is clearly getting himself ready to officiate by putting on his spotless white kurta and Nehru cap [FIG. II2].

RG This next spinning-of-thread shot in the gully above Manikarnika [FIG. II3] was an effort to bring in other aspects of the locale and also, more specifically, to suggest something with the thread image. Here is this long, frail thread being spun with enormous care by an old man as he crouches on a wall. I hoped that the Greek idea of a thread of life would come to mind as one watched this delicate undertaking.

I hope that no one fails to see the return of the chickadee or sparrow in this shot of the Dom Raja [FIG. II4]. You remember that this bird is almost totemic of this baleful person. There is a good deal of incongruity to this pairing, but that is the way it was. At least I didn't capture sparrows and release them whenever I wanted them in a shot of the Dom Raja, the way Herzog got the monkeys into *Aguirre.*

FIG. 114

ÁÖ I'm not quite sure why it's always striking to see this tiny bird with a forbidding, powerful figure like that. Somehow the little bird is either indifferent or really in league with that whale of a man.

RG At least, they are strange bedfellows. I'm reminded of a great shark kept company by a tiny pilot fish, or a bird waiting to pick the teeth of a hippopotamus.

ÁÖ It is well for us, and the sparrow, to remember that this man can, at the drop of a hat, be violent and aggressive, though he would probably do nothing to disturb the bird.

RG You mean he could wipe it out with the flick of his wrist?

ÁÖ Yes, but now, in the twentieth century, we have gotten used to a kind of sentimentality coexisting with brutality.

RG The audience may remember the cages of song birds that were kept at the Dom Raja's house. There was, at sunrise, an enormous twittering and chirping of birds at his house. I don't think it was ever loud enough to wake him, but they will always be associated with him in my mind.

ÁÖ Yes, and he spoke with great affection about his animals, including the freshwater alligators he had, and the rams, buffalo, and cows he kept in the house.

RG Some of which he wanted to barbecue for us.

ÁÖ So he was a complex and strangely modern man.

rg At this point in the film, many of the mysteries of Manikarnika gradually diminish, and the curtains are being steadily drawn back to show the place for what it really is. One of the things to be seen are the many members of the Dom Raja's caste who do all the work, the ones who sift the ashes, haul the water, split the wood, and just generally look after things.
We're about midway now into the last third of the film. The material we've been looking at most recently, such as glimpses of the Dom Raja putting on his white Nehru hat and sitting majestically in his little gallery above the ghats, has been about

FIG. 115

FIG. 116

FIG. 117

Manikarnika. This is followed by some shots of his minions doing various things, including sweeping the continuously mounting debris that is collecting on the steps that lead down to the river.

AÖ   After these shots of daily routine, we are suddenly confronted with the unique situation of a group of mourners.

RG   Yes, and it is the shot following the people sifting through the ashes down at the shore and the man sweeping the top of the wall descending the ghat [FIG. 115] that offers us another glimpse of that almost mythical denizen of this place, the water buffalo, who, to the accompaniment of a lament on the track, swivels a sad eye towards the camera [FIG. 116]. It's hard to tell whether it's the cry of a man or woman, but it doesn't really matter. It is so obviously a lament. Then the next shot is where one sees that it is a man and that he's very distressed [FIG. 117]. It was rather rare to see this, wasn't it? I mean, we didn't often see either men or women, for that matter, showing this kind of grief.

AÖ   Yes, I know, and I remember that you were somewhat bewildered by the customarily cool and restrained demeanor; it made it difficult to register people's emotions. However, it is the culturally approved thing not to exhibit too much attachment or overt grief, which would only detain the soul on its journey. Still, it does come through.

RG   Yes, it surges up every once in a while because loss is loss, even in the midst of cultural sanctions and limitations.

AÖ   Often the people who are most affected don't even come to the burning ground. At times, the widow or the widower stays either at a distance or doesn't come at all. Women, especially, may choose not to come to the burning ground. This lends a matter-of-fact air that is supported by the busy nature of the place and the work of all the Dom Raja's various dependents in these proceedings.

RG   And the endless ritualizing has its mesmeric side. For me, as a filmmaker wanting to come to grips with the business of death and separation but so indoctrinated by a very different— that is, Western—attitude regarding these matters, it was all slightly unreal. I didn't, for example, know how to deal with Hindu notions of a happy death, such as being glad to die in Benares or relief at the prospect of escaping the cycle of rebirth. Then, and even now, I think of these as very largely inconceivable and visually incommunicable ideas. This was why I felt such relief on hearing that man weep at the ghats and to film him and, later on, some women who also wept in a small, slightly removed group. I really felt that they were a key to getting across the idea that these people are reacting somewhat the way we do and are experiencing some of the same feelings of loss.

AÖ   I'm sure that they just channel it all into different forms. It always struck me that the more ritualized an activity becomes, the more it seems to internally isolate the practitioner, making the individual less accessible. This may account for some of the difficulty in filming such activity; but I think that sorrow and loss are both present. It is expressed differently. The way it is not allowed to surface certainly demonstrates the power of these beliefs.

RG   We're now getting to a more intense scrutiny of this place, Ákos, which, I'm sure you remember, became a really central location for the film. It is one of the great power places of the world, I would suppose, and so it makes sense to give it some prominence in the film. In a way, the film begins by looking at it through some pretty obscuring mist from the far shore. Then bit by bit, the place is revealed, and, finally, this incredible space becomes familiar, if not completely explicable. One of the recurring thoughts I had while shooting at Manikarnika was that I should be careful to avoid simply documenting cremation. I also remember thinking that though it would be pretty tedious to have to watch an endlessly burning body, there was some possibility that an image of flames consuming flesh could become a mandala of sorts. I began a shot like that one day but never was comfortable with what I saw in the viewfinder, and nothing much ever came of it. I think that I felt all the time at Manikarnika that death had to be made interesting, that I had an obligation to all those corpses and should be thinking of ways of trying to preserve their dignity.

AÖ   Well, it is definitely a place that affects one strongly, and I did not expect to be allowed to work there. I mean, it is a place where one can't just turn up and hope for the best. Such an approach would only have invited a lot of trouble, which we made a considerable effort to avoid. Nevertheless, I was quite surprised when everything fell into place and we found ourselves on the ghat itself. Given all that, and the fact that it was done in such an indirect manner, it still took us almost two weeks to accomplish.

RG   **A long time, a long time.**

AÖ   So, with hindsight, would you say it could have been done from farther away, say from the river, with long lenses?

RG   **No, I think one had to be in there to get at its intensity. This intensity, though, has very little to do with the fact that bodies are burned. This, as I've tried to say, is almost a detail, something that has to be done but in itself is of no great interest. I'm pretty confident that avoiding any straight-on gazing at this activity was the right thing, cinematically, to do.**

AÖ   Yes, because staring is not what you do even when you visit this place without a camera. In a way, you can understand why it's a place for meditation, because you don't really process what is happening until later. In a place like this, your mind is attending to some more interior agenda.

   I was very ambivalent throughout the time up on the ghat. In some ways it was an extraordinary time that I'll never forget, very powerful and very conducive to reflection. At other times, I felt very much an intruder.

RG   **Well, I guess that's why some of the more adventurous saddhus go there in order to live their deaths. They really impressed me, the ones that lay down on the wood at night to experience immolation. I also recall being told that one group of saddhus practiced cannibalism in an effort to get transgressively beyond all social convention. That's impressive.**

AÖ   I think it was lucky that we were granted all those permissions. It meant that we were included despite our alien looks and habits. When we were challenged—and this did happen because photography was prohibited there—we could say that we were a part of the proceedings, even if only temporarily. After a while, something seemed to draw us in and make us feel a part of the scene, and though it was full of ambivalence, it was a very rich experience.

RG   I very much agree that this powerful place puts the mind into a state of both reverie and amazement. It would have been impossible to just look on unthinkingly. Maybe this can help explain the construction of the film. The film is not touristic, because it couldn't be and still respect the actuality it is apprehending. An example of the kind of cinematic meditation that I'm suggesting is the quite extensive passage that deals with the sick puppy making an effort to climb the stairs [FIG. 118].
I can remember catching sight of this forlorn creature out of the corner of my eye and being immediately moved by the fact that it was unable to negotiate the steps. It was for this reason alone that so much time was spent getting the image and giving it a place in the film. Pretty clearly, it is not part of any ritual or daily routine. Its reason for being in the film has to do exclusively with its impact as an image.

FIG. 118

FIG. 119

AÖ   The scene that follows, of the men bringing a corpse down the steps on a litter [FIG. 119], shot from the point of view of the Dom Raja who sits framed by two columns, is quite effective. One of the men who comes down salutes us as he walks past, and this suggests a complicity with what's going on. So the feeling I have of what was happening on that ghat is that it was the process of, really, one's own death and regeneration, one's own cremation.

RG   Yes, without actually lying down on a pile of wood or eating some of the unburnt human leftovers, I think that everybody who goes there is something of an apprentice saddhu, insofar as there is any living through these preoccupations. I don't see how you can escape it. And then the question is what happens to a film that is connected with or even driven by that kind of concern, and I guess that's what we have here. I suppose I'm asking the usual question of how the nonfiction film can survive the presumed conflict between personal issues and informational or anthropological ones. This never occurred to me while I was shooting and only rarely in the editing.

FIG. 120

Here comes a case in point: the shot of the Dom Raja having an enormous argument with some mourners [FIG. 120]. Often people ask me why I didn't subtitle this sequence, and all I can say is that I thought what was being said was pretty obvious. Subtitles clearly would have provided more specific information, but the sequence would not have conveyed the same tone because the subtitling would have influenced the way it was seen.

AÖ   This is an interesting question, because so far we have had a lot of universality in the Manikarnika sequence. But here is an incident that particularizes things, and, therefore, maybe the same rules don't apply.

RG   It is very particular, yes . . . idiosyncratic perhaps.

AÖ   So when you placed it here, what were you thinking?

RG   I'm not sure, except that I liked the expression of arrogant contempt on the part of the Dom Raja. It gave him more dimension as a figure. There he was losing his regal cool and telling off a client who was trying to get his corpse in for less money. I was never able to do much with the Dom Raja; so this was an opportunity to see him with his hair down, so to speak. The question remains, though, of whether it is good filmmaking. By leaving it in I have opened the door to questions of what is being said, because audiences see and hear this long, contentious interchange and start feeling like they should know more. They don't realize that there is not that much being said. If you are asking me now what my thinking is about this being in the film, I would say maybe it should not be there, just because people sometimes feel frustrated when they see it.

AÖ   It would be quite different and perhaps less justified if it weren't for the earlier appearances of the Dom Raja. I mean, if it were just a sequence at Manikarnika that happened to have him in it without our previous encounters with him, it would make much less sense.

RG   Yes, he has been established pretty well already, and, I guess, the question is really whether this scene helps this process along. It was never my intention to do so-called "portraits" of any of our main figures. I didn't want the film to fall into that genre trap.

ÁÖ   The other interesting question is the perennial one of just how another person is to be filmed.

RG   I guess you are inquiring into the business of what gives a true account of someone and what distorts or simply comes up short. Documenting a person, or personality, seems even more problematic to me than documenting a ritual or some other activity. It seems to me that all of our own private views of another person are total fictions, yet somehow functional when it comes to knowing that other person. The very idea of finding a way to reproduce some reality that can be called another person is, on its face, a total absurdity. The same is true for behavior. One of my anthropology professors once said that the only thing real about culture is that it is always changing. I'm sure I heard the same thing from my psychoanalyst about personality. Think how handicapped film is in its fixedness. I suspect that this is part of the explanation for why so many old films look so quaint and peculiar. They haven't changed, but everything else has.

ÁÖ   I think what I had in mind was that the Dom Raja wasn't being shortchanged in this process, because he did assent to all this, and he knew very well that we were filming this particular sequence.

RG   It is the ethics that you are getting at, then. How much of a victim is someone like the Dom Raja?

ÁÖ   He made no attempt to stop the filming, which is maybe a way of saying that he wanted to be seen this way, that this behavior was a part of his own self-image. He did ask that we not film certain things.

RG   He was quite determined that we not show anything about his bookkeeping at the ghat.

ÁÖ   Yes, he had a lot of tax trouble and a negative press in India.

RG   I think he wanted to demonstrate his entrepreneurial skills, and I also think he was acting to the hilt in this little sequence.

AÖ   Also, back at his house, when he was dressing to leave the compound, he was in a way directing the filming himself.

RG   **You mean by letting you see what he wanted you to see and by creating long periods of inaction?**

AÖ   It was mostly passive, but he also made demands where he felt his well-being, in terms of livelihood, was at stake, and I think those were all honored.

RG   **Totally, with the exception of some gray areas where he was not aware that the camera was being used, such as when he was asleep.**

AÖ   It may be that he has come through in ways that repulse people a bit, but I think these ways would have appealed to him because they show him as a powerful presence.

RG   **Yes, he certainly wanted to project an image of strength. His obviously failing health was undermining those intentions, though. Still, he did seem in some strange way suited to a life of commanding others.**

AÖ   Another strange part about this is that some people come away with the idea of a really vulgar, disgusting but powerful man, and so they would see only the seamy side of the business of death. It never struck me that way, I must say. I know that the Dom Raja could and did exploit his position. I also know that many local people didn't want to take him seriously and couldn't handle his being so prominent in the affairs of Benares. It would have been interesting to see what happened in the wake of his death, which, as you know, occurred shortly after we left Benares. Incidentally, the amounts they are haggling over are small, but they meant a lot to everyone involved. I guess for the Dom Raja, and also for the little people who are overawed by him, a few pennies make all the difference. On the whole, it is something the local people handle better than those from the outside. In another sense, the supposedly "terrible" business of death is all very much in the open. It is more open than in our society, where the mercantile aspect is carefully hidden.

RG   **Yes, hidden by gentility and suavity, which pretty much obliterate the whole transaction, not to mention most of the feelings surrounding it.**

FIG. 121

FIG. 122

ÁÖ This next scene here, where the "set," as it were, of Manikarnika Ghat is being repainted [FIG. 121], is also a telling one.

RG Yes, there is a general cleanup, which I actually thought at the time was in response to the camera having come into the situation. The Dom Raja was making an effort at appearances, I think. These ladies who are diligently poking through the dying embers of the fires [FIG. 122] absolutely fascinated me. I was often tempted to spend some time just trying to understand what it was that they were doing, and yet I don't think I got very far. It was so ambiguous as far as I was concerned. I still don't know whether they were trying to find jewelry or coins or whether they were getting out pieces of charcoal for their home fires.

ÁÖ Charcoal mostly. I didn't follow it up, but they were often chased away by the doms. They were allowed a certain amount of charcoal, but it was kept account of by the Dom Raja's minions.

RG It reminded me of starving peasants gleaning the scraps after the harvest.

ÁÖ Yes, or people who look for spillage from trains carrying coal. I'm not sure what the understanding is between them and the Dom Raja.

RG In a way, this next section is an attempt, in something approximating real time, to give an account of the daily activities at Manikarnika. People are just going about their business, the Dom Raja is having his midday meal, and everything is really quite normal. That is, if anything can be thought of as normal in a place like this. How can it be normal and so powerful at the same time? How can it be tedious to watch some of the things that are happening there, knowing that it is the focus of such enormously intense goings-on?

ÁÖ This sequence of the Dom Raja eating shows just how alert and cognizant he is of everything. I mean, his glances are taking in

FIG. 123

FIG. 124

the whole place [FIG. 123]. Here is a real shift from one aspect of his character to another.

RG The next scene starts another sequence. It is in Mithai Lal's house, where he is performing a healing ritual for some people who have come for his help [FIG. 124]. This parallels the Dom Raja sequence we've just been looking at. I suppose you could say, "Meanwhile, back at Mithai Lal's, religious life goes on in another way." The idea of the sequence is to make people aware of yet more gestures made to bring about some desired result. Again, it is hard for me to be sure that an audience looking at something as strange as some of this will know what is happening. I still don't know what exactly Mithai Lal was doing with those bits of his broken clay cup. I assumed at the time that he was using them in some form of divination. I think that if the pieces remained attached to the pointed fragment he stuck into them it meant one thing, and if they didn't it meant the opposite. At the time I wasn't really very concerned about it. It didn't matter to me that I didn't know in detail what he was doing. I felt strongly that I knew why he was doing what he was doing, that this odd business had to do with trying to help someone.

ÁÓ   What is interesting for me is just what comes across of Mithai Lal, who in some ways is the most ambiguous character. We see him in such different roles: as a ritualist, as a healer, as a seer.

FIG. 125

Maybe all of these activities come together to create a sense of good about the man, that he cannot do harm. In a way he can, though. He can use these powers to smite people. The other thing that just struck me now watching this is that what happens in the frame takes on a significance because it follows directly upon the Dom Raja's outburst of anger. Here we get a burst of ambiguous laughter [FIG. 125].

RG   I like to think of it as a cosmic cackle. Which is to say, perhaps, that it is both very elevated and very ordinary at the same time.

AÖ   Exactly. Which is also to say that it is not quite clear whom or what he is laughing at.

RG   I think that was intentional on his part. It certainly was on mine.

AÖ   Yes?

RG   Oh, definitely.

AÖ   Of course, it's completely in character. In his last scenes at the Durga temple, you can see that he also has these seemingly unprovoked bursts of anger and screaming, by which only strangers are really taken in.

RG   Yes, he is definitely on an edge in the way he functions. It has to be part of his bag of tricks as a healer to be able to inhabit, or at least to summon up, two quite different emotional environments.

AÖ   Even though his manner is essentially benign, it must impress a stranger; but that, in turn, seems to be in character with what you expect of holy men. They are unpredictable and they do strange things.

RG   Isn't that their principal stock in trade?

AÖ   This peculiarity of his is consciously evoked in the film by the sound of his laughter, which, as I recall, was occasioned by something in the manner of the man who was worshiping at his shrine. I also think he dragged it out to attract attention, being the performer that he is.

RG   Well, I wouldn't put it past him, but I doubt that anyone except us would have that insight into his personality. Certainly the film is not going to inform anyone as to this.

AÖ   It's very telling, the way he proceeds in the sight of his god and goddess.

RG   I like the wonderfully casual relationship between Mithai Lal and his gods and goddesses. That everything could be on such a friendly basis seemed to me to make a lot of sense. You know, it's a lesson that would be well worth learning from the film, if it were possible to point to that moral in some way.

AÖ   So the film, at this point, seems both to develop him as a character, just like the Dom Raja, and also to add a mythical aspect.

FIG. 126

RG But don't forget this edge of insanity that he conjures with. What does it mean to laugh in the presence of one's deities?

AÖ   Then, again, there's this characteristic drawing in of breath and shaking, and then immediately he's off on a different quest. There is no more nonsense, and he shifts from consulting the oracle to healing. Now, this is probably an unmistakable gesture. Wouldn't you say?

RG I would hope, yes, so that the film can make the point that he is a healer without having to say it in a voice-over or in subtitles.

AÖ   That he is in fact laying hands on [FIG. 126] . . .

FIG. 127

RG Exactly, yes. I mean, what can people do to each other as healer and patient except lay hands on, spit on, blow on, or some such thing? There are just so many possibilities, physically speaking, for making a curing gesture towards another person, and the fact that many religions should end up with people putting hands on each other doesn't seem to me at all strange. So the cut is to a shot, once again, of Manikarnika, where things start to reintensify in a montage of images cut with somewhat more rapid pacing.

AÖ   Yes, and, as you said before, many of the steps, the actual ritual procedures, are right here for anyone who wants to puzzle out their sequence.

FIG. 128

MAKING **FOREST OF BLISS**

FIG. 129

FIG. 130

RG That's right. At this point, in fact, you're beginning to see something that is quite sequential as far as these things are concerned. A body is brought down and immersed in the river [FIG. 127]. Then it is put on the steps to wait [FIG. 128] until there is a place to burn it and the wood is gathered, piled up, and so forth.

ÁÖ Then the chief mourner takes coals from the sacred fire [FIG. 129].

RG Right, it's the same sacred fire that's first seen from the farther shore in the prologue: the same fire that burns all the time. And now we're in the midst of its sacredness and hopefully not wondering what it means.

This next shot is an interesting one for me because I was never sure during the editing that I wanted to use it. This is one of the last scenes in this montage of cremation activities, and it shows a huge foreground expanse of a boat at the river's edge [FIG. 130]. In the background we see Manikarnika and a chief mourner who, after circumambulating the funeral pyre, ignites the pyre at the end of the shot. Now, I don't know whether this really works, but it certainly contains all the elements I was looking for: namely, the boat, the river, fire, and a soul being dispatched. The boat seemed to be waiting on the shore for the crossing. It's a kind of summary shot which, if inspected at all carefully, contains a tremendous amount of information.

ÁÖ Yes, and this is actually one strategy for filming ritual. But it is not the only solution, or maybe even a very good one. We have been discussing over the years how difficult it is to deal cinematically with ritual, which has its own structure. But this is certainly one way of evoking the totality of it and dealing with it, not as a monograph would but as a film would, and this kind of film at that. At the same time, there is no reason why one can't extract the essential information, if that's what one wants to do. Other things may also be happening, but on the level of fidelity, the film is faithful to the actual events as far as they are apprehensible. The fact that there is a subjective element in their apprehension doesn't mean that the thing isn't there.

RG   Not unless one wants to be completely skeptical of the world. As far as filming ritual is concerned, I don't really think special rules apply, since it seems to me ritual is still behavior. It may have its own structure and be more predictable, but this might actually be helpful to the filmmaker. When we find a way to get at the form, content, and meaning of actuality, we will also have found a way to film ritual. Of course, there will not be one way but a succession of ways discovered by different people grappling with these problems down through time.

ÁÖ   The sounds in this particular scene are also quite significant. They are fairly quiet. You hear a couple of dogs, the fire, water dripping, and a few other vaguely human noises that are very soft in the background. The effect is the opposite of so much that has gone on until now.

RG   Yes, it is a big change from the tumult of so much else that one has been hearing. There is also an intention here to strike a note of tranquility, to suggest a lull following something like a storm.

ÁÖ   It is followed by two closer shots. The first, a shot of a boy drinking casually from a broken pipe, with cremation fires in the background, combines the everyday and ordinary with the extraordinary. Then follows the first really explicit close-up of a burning body [FIG. 131].

FIG. 131

RG   Yes, this is the first time that anyone actually sees cremation, a discernible body being consumed by discernible flames. This is the only time in the film that the audience is asked to see this way—passively, I would say, since there is nothing being asked of anyone except that they keep their eyes open. I was very concerned when I was doing this, and I remember this part as the hardest of the film to edit. The rest of the film, by comparison, really almost edited itself. That's obviously not true, but it felt that way because it had a remarkable feeling of inevitability to it. But this part was very problematic, very difficult, and I wasn't sure what I should do. The whole Manikarnika episode in the film had to end in a way that resulted in some understanding and that also created some useful mystery. I worked a long time to get it to satisfy these two requirements.

ÁÖ   Well, I'm not sure. Here I find myself almost unequivocally on the other side, in the sense that it could have gone on much longer. The fire somehow makes it look more abstract. You weren't reticent about the earlier glimpses of corpses in the river and so forth, which have a far more recognizable and candid aspect. This body is somewhat screened by the fire.

RG   **It has something to do with the obviousness of what is happening. I mean, when you set fire to something that's combustible, it's going to burn up. That's not only pretty obvious, it is completely unambiguous. But you are right about the possibility of abstraction, the fire screening the body, and so forth. A lot depends on how the shot is made, what the camera does to the subject. I think I may not have been too resourceful here.**

ÁÖ   This scene of the Dom Raja's assistants is one of the saddest imaginable in that one clearly sees all that is left of somebody: the garments still wet from the ritual dip in the Ganges and the few personal ornaments that by custom belong to the doms.

FIG. 132

RG   **Yes, there is this awful sense of a life having vanished, leaving virtually no trace, nothing but these pathetic little objects remaining to mark its passing, and then they get kicked off the edge of the porch into the dust and ashes** [FIG. 132].

ÁÖ   The rags suggest hospital to me.

RG   **I'm reminded of Yeats's "rag and bone shop of the heart."**

ÁÖ   Then there is a series of shorter shots: the sacred fire, the bracelet, and the bird, too.

RG   **Yes, the sparrow has come back to the Dom Raja. It's really his totem, as I was saying earlier.**
     At this point there is a lament of some women who gathered on the roof of the Dom Raja's porch in a little balcony where they could be relatively inconspicuous. When I edited this, I hoped that the connection would be made between the lady's bracelet and the ladies' lament, almost as if everyone had known each other.
     These are the last scenes of the Dom Raja. It's a pretty starkly real business getting that needle into his bottom. Nothing

FIG. 133

mythical there. The shot is meant to make him more real and to provide ironic contrast: the merchant of death trying to keep his own ravaged body alive.

The next cut is important, and it is one with which I had great difficulty. It is the beginning of a transition from Manikarnika to the rest of the city and to a larger context. The cut is to a very lyrical shot of birds pecking at some seeds on a parapet above the ghat, with the Ganges in the background [FIG. 133]. The editing problem was finding a way to get out of this powerful place. What I mean is that I had the feeling I couldn't and shouldn't stay there any longer: beyond a certain point, it doesn't make sense to keep looking at even powerful things. One has to breathe a little, perhaps grieve a little. Above all, distance is required for the meditation that you spoke of earlier. So here are the sparrows, some seeds, and a funeral pot.

AÖ   The pot itself is important.

FIG. 134

RG   So that was the penultimate shot, just before the final reprise of Manikarnika Ghat. I think there are nine or ten key images of Manikarnika in a relatively fast-paced montage that recapitulates what has been seen over a major section of the film. It ends with a chief mourner throwing a pot over his shoulder, smashing it on the ground [FIG. 134]. This scene suggested to me the parable about the pot that's broken at the well. Actually, this short section contains a great deal of new as well as familiar information.

AÖ   It does get pretty explicit.

RG   Yes, and then it returns to the lyrical idiom that began with the parapet, birds, seeds, and pot. Finally, it is to be fondly hoped, one has gotten out of the powerful circle of the Great Burning Ground.

AÖ   In that montage you have included a shot of a skull being broken to release the spirit [FIG. 135].

FIG. 135

MAKING **FOREST OF BLISS**

FIG. 136

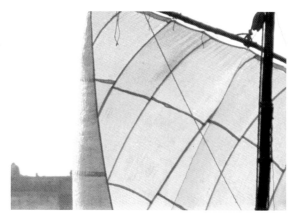

FIG. 137

FIG. 138

RG Yes, that is right, but not many people know that the skull is broken there in that sequence. It was a conscious choice, obviously, to put it in as a very short fragment rather than to use it in its entirety, which would mean seeing the head being beaten and beaten by one of the long bamboo litter poles until it finally cracks open and the brains pop out. This way it's there and it's not there.

ÁÖ I think that it will come home to people that the pot-breaking is the last act in a series of rituals at the cremation ground. There is such a finality to this, and it has so many rich ritual connotations. It really does draw a line here. Then we go back to the river and the circling dogs [FIG. 136].

RG Yes, we're on the "far shore" again, only, in contrast to the beginning of the film, when boats were going down river, the movement is now up river, against the current [FIG. 137]. There was a possibility here, I thought, to support the film's cyclical structure by having the motion come back the other way.

ÁÖ It's curious that right in front of Benares itself, the river makes a turn to the north so that what would normally be up river and down river is reversed; so you are getting a reversal of a reversal.

RG Many times I did not know if I was going up or down that river.

ÁÖ It is almost the end of the day here. It is dusk, and the image is of a little boy flying his kite [FIG. 138].

RG . . . which is another echo from the prologue, where the kite is first seen at the break of day, pulling up the sun, I think I said. Here the little boys are pulling it down. Most importantly, this section is meant to encourage the association between life,

FIG. 139

FIG. 140

including death, and kites. It's particularly apparent, I hope, when one looks carefully at the sequence of shots of the boat that drifts out to deposit a child's body in the river [FIG. 139].

ÅÖ This image is one of the strongest, I think, in the whole film.

RG I am sure you remember how much time I spent trying to film a kite falling into the river. I didn't know, at the time, exactly why I wanted that image. I thought that filming kites was something I could do until I saw a more promising direction in which to take the film. There was also some obscure feeling that kites drifting off toward the far shore and sometimes falling into the river had a larger meaning. They are wonderful inventions: so frail, so lively, and so urgent. Then there is the string that both guides and attaches them but that can also break and release them. So it does not seem so strange to me now that I spent so much time with the kites. I can remember thinking that their flight was only part of it. You must also have the kite falling and expiring in the water.

I tried for a long time to get the kite to fall where I wanted, and I don't think I ever really got it until I was doing something else. It was just the same with the dolphins that eluded me for weeks until I was shooting something else and one surfaced in the frame, much to our mutual surprise, I am sure.

Here, in the shot where a body is being dropped in the river, a kite falls in the background. So, as the body is put in, the kite joins it. You know, the whole thing seems to get said in one quite simple symbolic passage that is, at the same time, power-fully actual. This was great luck, and someday we should ask ourselves what proportion of nonfiction film proceeds from luck. But now let me follow along with what is happening here as I remember it. The kite sequence has brought the "far shore" idea into real focus, I trust, and as the body and the kite both start their journeys to that shore, the scene cut is to a water buffalo [FIG. 140]. This is a very deliberate and even abrupt cut. The thing that struck me in this shot is the sad eye of this huge beast.

FIG. 141

FIG. 142

FIG. 143

What I wanted was for that eye to give a melancholy look at what had just happened. There are actually two shots of the huge beast. The body is put in, the boat drifts, the kite falls in the water, and this wet, sad eye of the buffalo swings toward the camera; in the second shot, the animal climbs the steps of the ghat leading up to the city [FIG. 141]. And that is a whole, complete little episode in the film. We—and the buffalo too, I guess—return to a life that goes endlessly on.

This next series of shots, in the marigold gardens [FIG. 142], should by now be thoroughly recognizable. It is a harking back to the marigold theme, to a time in the beginning of the marigold cycle, or story, of irrigation and cultivation. So it is also a restatement of the idea of circularity in things organic.

AÖ We are right in front of the Durga temple as people are going inside and ringing bells to call the gods' attention to their acts of devotion.

RG It seemed to me, after all the Manikarnika business and the really quite touching scenes of the child being put into the river, terribly important to come up with some affirmation of life. In any case, that was the reasoning behind going into the temple [FIG. 143] and seeing people reveal their desire to live better lives and to come closer to their god. It was important to show that life is not just one loss or sorrow after another.

AÖ Yes, again these are very rich human situations that are charged with all kinds of meaning and possibility. This temple is also a power place, offering many potential rewards. For me, just to be there had a regenerating effect. I liked being there simply taking everything in: the monkeys, the people, the gods, the incense. This particular sequence shows all this and a brief look at some of the men who come to renew their powers as healers or disciples.

<u>RG</u>   The man who prostrates himself over the firepit was pretty intense. I was very unhappy when I ran out of film just as he was reaching the peak of his ecstasy. But that is only a small part of the difficulty of nonfiction filmmaking.

<u>AÖ</u>   He was being enlivened by divine energy at the place of the homa, the sacred fire sacrifice which, though not active as a fire ritual at this particular moment, is still a place full of the potential of the sacrifice. Everything that happens in the temple compound has to do with physical gestures: touching objects, lighting lamps, and prostrating oneself. This is not an organized ritual in the sense of something conducted by a priest; these are people worshiping in their own personal way.

FIG. 144

<u>RG</u>   At the end of the temple sequence, the cut is to a courtyard at another temple where two girls are playing hopscotch [FIG. 144]. Here is another moment of affirmation in which one sees youth and vitality, even a touch of joy. There is also the game's conceptual and historic framework; I have been told that this game, like parcheesi and chess, is a cosmic paradigm. Specifically, it is a ladder up which one strives to reach heaven. Now, I don't really expect people to bring any knowledge of this into their view-ing, but I am intrigued by the idea that some dim comprehension flickers in the cultural memories of a few who are watching. In any case, it is nice to think of children having something to say about the destiny of the world. I suppose it could be left at that. I would certainly not try to instruct anyone in these arcane matters; hence, there are no subtitles and there is no narration. What I did do when I shot the scene was to use slow motion, which was meant only to inflect the image, to say that this scene should be looked at slightly differently than others.

<u>AÖ</u>   We actually found two local names for this game: one was "crossing the ocean"; the other was "reaching the island."

<u>RG</u>   The cut after the girls playing hopscotch is to the film's central geographic location, the river. The little girls have made their singular statements of delight in play, and the film resumes its exploration of the significance of a great phenomenon of nature. It occurs to me that the film will, from here until it ends,

stay close to the river. In a way, the film comes back to that with which it began.

AÖ   Actually, this is a traveling shot past Harishchandra Ghat, the other burning ground, and there is a fallen and broken kite in the foreground.

RG   Yes, that is right. One sometimes forgets there is more than one cremation ground.

AÖ   The shot following the boy flying his kite always struck me as a particularly long, quiet, yet strange dusk or sunset scene.

RG   You mean the one of the boat on the river with the flattened city in the distance?

AÖ   It's the one with the big red sun and the boat going down river. Then the boat goes out of the frame and the camera just sits there.

RG   That's right, except at the end of the shot a monkey climbs up on the parapet of a house [FIG. 145], and it made me think that the city was being taken over at twilight by another species, maybe even by Octavio Paz's *singes grammariens*.

FIG. 145

AÖ   The monkey? Was it the monkey that interested you, or did you just feel that this quiet moment should be held?

RG   I did feel that there should be a pause before the film went into its final sequences, but I also thought the monkey afforded a wonderfully surrealistic comment on the whole urban panorama. The monkey could be saying, if monkeys only said things more clearly, that this world we are in is actually being watched over by relatives of a lower order. There is also the pleasure I took in the pure accident of the shot. I had begun the shot intending to film the skyline at dusk, and, suddenly, an incredible ship sails into the frame. Then, moments later, a mischievous great monkey climbs out of the city, onto the roof of the tallest building. How can such gifts of actuality be rejected? Even if the monkey is not going to solve our problems or reduce our perplexity, I could not resist the joke it was playing by simply being there. Nor could

FIG. 146

FIG. 147

I resist this next scene of the arati at the Durga temple [FIG. 146]. It's there really as a prelude to Mithai Lal's performance at what you are calling the homa pit.

AÖ What he's doing is called "ghi chara," which means that he is pouring clarified butter into the fire [FIG. 147]. This gesture is on behalf of all those people who brought the ghi in order to please the Goddess. It is a way of giving thanks or asking for a boon. These are the people who came to Mithai Lal's house during the week and are now visiting the temple on the day he is making offerings to the Goddess.

RG What interested me here, as a filmmaker, was that edge I have spoken of between sanity and insanity that Mithai Lal approaches. It is a place that we must be led to by such a man because we do not have the courage or the ability to get there on our own. At this point, my job really becomes one of trying to get across his performance, since that, quite clearly, is what he is giving with considerable competence. I don't mean that there is any lack of sincerity in what he is doing. I only mean that he wants his actions to have a certain look, and I, in turn, wanted to capture it; hence the effort I made to get that quality of craziness in his voice and the hint of madness in his eyes.

AÖ His particular state is certainly brought out in these scenes. This state, incidentally, is one that I am frequently asked about by people, who want to know whether he is "really" in trance—a question that seems to me wholly inappropriate. The real point is that he is in a condition, altered or otherwise, which is fully exciting him and which creates a link between the Goddess, his patients, and himself.

RG Well, I suspect the people who ask those kinds of questions would like to have an answer in the affirmative. They would like to be sure he is in what they think is a trance so that he will be "explained" and they will no longer need to pay quite the same kind of attention to him.

AÖ   Yes, they want a rational explanation of a nonrational act. Yet these close-ups confound those expectations, because we really are not privy to his experience. We see the signs of it and to some extent can share it, but only as much as one can without entering through practice.

RG   But isn't this the sleight of hand we're trying to practice? Finding ways to get at other people's experience. In any case, the scene is once again a boat on the river [FIG. 148]. The sun is rising for the second time to frame the whole film in the structure of a day that ends only to start again. The remainder of the film is devoted to Ragul Pandit—the coolest, wisest, and most worldly of the film's three citizens of Benares. He will give a final benediction here at the end of the film, not just to the people who are in the shrine but, if it isn't too presumptuous, to everyone who is watching the film. People in the audience have been through a relatively unsparing account of some of life's fundamental issues, and they deserve it.

FIG. 148

AÖ   There was nothing special about this occasion. It was just an aspect of everyday life, quite modest in its display of religious feeling.

RG   I suppose we might have gone to the Visvanath temple and arranged for a "High Hindu Mass."

AÖ   But the understated quality of the devotion here [FIG. 149] is what reinforces its conviction and justifies its position in the film.

FIG. 149

RG   Well, the intention from the start was to avoid the gaudy and theatrical, because it seemed so much less compelling.

AÖ   Yes, I know. A lot of rituals got left out.

RG   . . . to be included somewhere else, perhaps, but not here. I did wonder sometimes if things were not getting somewhat thin. I even worried that maybe there wasn't enough energy to sustain a feature-length treatment. But I no longer feel that way. In fact, I now sometimes worry that the film is too intense, too rich.

FIG. 150

FIG. 151

FIG. 152

ÁÖ In the end it was conviction in the work on the gods' behalf that pulled it through. Ragul Pandit's gestures here, for example, were not only part of a routine ritual, they were personally felt.

RG Of the three figures, I think he was the most transparent, so I probably would have been able to detect any lack of sincerity.

ÁÖ All of these things we just mentioned rescue the sequence from being the portrayal of simply an ordinary, repetitive, and formal act. Here the worship comes out as something unique, and it's not even particularly musical as an expression.

RG You know, I actually was very moved by it. I really like hearing this passage. It's not exactly Gregorian chant, but an equivalent, maybe.

ÁÖ Ragulji himself remarked that usually there are more people and the singing is a bit more forceful.

RG It is now, during this final sequence in the shrine and especially in the ending shot, that the last pieces of the puzzle are put in place. You see the dismantling of the bamboo litter [FIG. 150], a prowling dog [FIG. 151], and a wood barge [FIG. 152] as cutaways from the shrine. But it is the long, last shot of mist on the river and that ghostly boat being rowed across the screen and out of sight [FIG. 153] that brings the film back to the point at which it began. The only permanence seems to be the necessity of beginning again—that and the sound of the oarlocks.

FIG. 153

Shot List **Forest of Bliss**

FIG #	PAGE #	SHOT #	DESCRIPTION	SHOT BEGINS				SHOT LENGTH	
				0 hr	0 min	sec	frame #	sec	frames
FIG. 1	p.16	1	Long fade-in to a running dog			0 sec	frame #0	25 sec	16 frames
FIG. 2	p.17	2	Mist and boat on Ganges			25 sec	frame #16	20 sec	11 frames
FIG. 3	p.18	3	Hawk on far shore			45 sec	frame #27	2 sec	18 frames
FIG. 4	p.19	4	Mist and boat on Ganges from far shore			48 sec	frame #15	23 sec	15 frames
FIG. 5	p.19	5	Sand workers on far shore in mist		1 min	12 sec	frame #0	14 sec	6 frames
FIG. 6	p.19	6	Boy runs with kite on far shore			26 sec	frame #6	4 sec	25 frames
FIG. 7	p.20	7	Huge rising sun from far shore			31 sec	frame #1	5 sec	21 frames
FIG. 8	p.20	8	Steps with corpse at Manikarnika from far shore			36 sec	frame #22	8 sec	2 frames
FIG. 9	p.20	9	Boat on Ganges passes left to right from far shore			44 sec	frame #24	12 sec	17 frames
FIG. 10	p.21	10	Sacred fire from far shore			57 sec	frame #11	6 sec	14 frames
FIG. 11	p.22	11	Dogs fight on far shore		2 min	3 sec	frame #25	15 sec	16 frames
		12	Fade in titles—Yeats quote			19 sec	frame #11	43 sec	29 frames
			Main title, "Forest of Bliss"						
			"A Film by Robert Gardner"						
			"Produced by . . ."						
			"Benares, India"						
FIG. 12	p.26	13	Fade in first scene— Mithai Lal leaves house		3 min	3 sec	frame #10	13 sec	12 frames
		14	Mithai Lal starts for morning bath			16 sec	frame #22	10 sec	5 frames
FIG. 13	p.27	15	Mithai Lal continues			26 sec	frame #27	5 sec	14 frames
		16	Mithai Lal starts down steps			32 sec	frame #11	5 sec	19 frames
FIG. 14	p.28	17	Mithai Lal goes past wood-weighing scales			38 sec	frame #0	5 sec	11 frames
		18	Mithai Lal continues			43 sec	frame #11	15 sec	5 frames
FIG. 15	p.29	19	Mithai Lal goes down narrow stairway			58 sec	frame #16	12 sec	21 frames
		20	Mithai Lal passes stack of wood		4 min	11 sec	frame #7	8 sec	18 frames
		21	Mithai Lal comes out above river			19 sec	frame #25	11 sec	15 frames
		22	Mithai Lal descends to river's edge			31 sec	frame #10	10 sec	24 frames
FIG. 16	p.30	23	Boat's sail going right to left			42 sec	frame #4	11 sec	15 frames
		24	Mithai Lal at edge of Ganges			53 sec	frame #19	34 sec	26 frames
FIG. 17	p.31	25	Close shot of offerings on Ganges		5 min	28 sec	frame #15	2 sec	24 frames
		26	Pilgrims make offerings of marigolds			31 sec	frame #9	11 sec	20 frames
FIG. 18	p.32	27	Mithai Lal swimming			42 sec	frame #29	43 sec	28 frames

FIG #	PAGE #	SHOT #	DESCRIPTION	SHOT BEGINS			SHOT LENGTH	
		28	Rising sun	0 hr 6 min	26 sec	frame #27	3 sec	10 frames
FIG. 19	P.33	29	Mithai Lal begins worship		30 sec	frame #7	31 sec	7 frames
FIG. 20	P.34	30	Dog gnaws at corpse at river's edge	7 min	1 sec	frame #14	9 sec	10 frames
FIG. 21	P.35	31	Bow of boat glides on river		10 sec	frame #24	2 sec	23 frames
FIG. 22	P.35	32	Mithai Lal offers water to sun		13 sec	frame #17	30 sec	20 frames
		33	Mithai Lal climbs out of water		44 sec	frame #7	12 sec	28 frames
		34	Mithai Lal lustrates deities		57 sec	frame #5	9 sec	7 frames
FIG. 23	P.35	35	Ringing huge bell at Dom Raja's	8 min	6 sec	frame #12	4 sec	0 frames
		36	Priest in Dom Raja's shrine		10 sec	frame #12	18 sec	9 frames
		37	Ringing bell		28 sec	frame #21	4 sec	15 frames
FIG. 24	P.36	38	Tiger and vultures from Dom Raja's balcony		33 sec	frame #6	8 sec	15 frames
		39	Dom Raja being massaged awake		41 sec	frame #21	13 sec	29 frames
		40	Tiger's mouth and vultures		55 sec	frame #20	10 sec	15 frames
		41	Dom Raja, closer shot	9 min	6 sec	frame #5	11 sec	29 frames
		42	Man sets out bird cages		18 sec	frame #4	10 sec	3 frames
FIG. 25	P.36	43	Dom Raja sleeps—cigarette burns		28 sec	frame #7	39 sec	24 frames
		44	Birds in cage	10 min	8 sec	frame #1	4 sec	23 frames
FIG. 26	P.37	45	Ragul Pandit, at river's edge, starts prayers		12 sec	frame #24	18 sec	17 frames
		46	Continuation—different angle		31 sec	frame #11	71 sec	24 frames
FIG. 27	P.40	47	Mithai Lal starts home	11 min	53 sec	frame #5	14 sec	24 frames
		48	Mithai Lal goes up the stair	12 min	7 sec	frame #29	6 sec	10 frames
		49	Mithai Lal dances		14 sec	frame #9	21 sec	11 frames
		50	Mithai Lal uses mirror		35 sec	frame #20	22 sec	6 frames
		51	Mithai Lal prays to river		57 sec	frame #26	12 sec	6 frames
		52	Mithai Lal ascends steps with wife	13 min	10 sec	frame #2	11 sec	25 frames
FIG. 28	P.41	53	Mithai Lal goes up more stairs and through gate		21 sec	frame #27	9 sec	17 frames
		54	Mithai Lal and beggars		31 sec	frame #14	9 sec	28 frames
		55	Same—different angle		41 sec	frame #12	0 sec	0 frames
FIG. 29	P.42	56	Mithai Lal up narrow stairway past sleeping figure		44 sec	frame #12	13 sec	9 frames
		57	Sleeping figure stirs		57 sec	frame #21	5 sec	25 frames
FIG. 30	P.43	58	Mithai Lal adorns lingams	14 min	3 sec	frame #16	59 sec	15 frames

FIG #	PAGE #	SHOT #	DESCRIPTION	SHOT BEGINS			SHOT LENGTH	
FIG. 31	p.43	59	Mithai Lal continues home past kite	0 hr 15 min	3 sec	frame #1	3 sec	26 frames
		60	Mithai Lal continues up stairway		6 sec	frame #27	10 sec	15 frames
		61	Mithai Lal sprinkles shrine		17 sec	frame #12	26 sec	29 frames
		62	Mithai Lal up more stairs		44 sec	frame #11	6 sec	16 frames
		63	Mithai Lal knocks head on stairs		50 sec	frame #27	5 sec	0 frames
FIG. 32	p.44	64	Mithai Lal approaches his house		55 sec	frame #27	6 sec	5 frames
FIG. 33	p.45	65	Medium shot man and marigolds	16 min	2 sec	frame #2	8 sec	25 frames
		66	Close-up face, man picking marigolds—tilt to head		10 sec	frame #27	2 sec	15 frames
		67	Close-up hands picking marigolds		13 sec	frame #12	10 sec	24 frames
		68	Closer hands picking marigolds		24 sec	frame #6	11 sec	18 frames
		69	Traveling shot of woman carrying basket of marigolds on head		35 sec	frame #24	15 sec	23 frames
		70	Following shot—same—into village		51 sec	frame #17	20 sec	4 frames
		71	Woman puts down basket of marigolds	17 min	11 sec	frame #21	4 sec	21 frames
FIG. 34	p.47	72	Man picks up enormous log		16 sec	frame #12	28 sec	24 frames
		73	Same action—different angle at Raj Ghat		45 sec	frame #6	11 sec	29 frames
		74	Same action—different angle at Raj Ghat		57 sec	frame #5	11 sec	24 frames
		75	Following shot—man carries wood to barge	18 min	8 sec	frame #29	5 sec	17 frames
		76	Different angle—same—traveling shot onto boat		14 sec	frame #16	17 sec	0 frames
FIG. 35	p.47	77	Huge log dumped into boat		31 sec	frame #16	5 sec	8 frames
		78	Same—different angle		36 sec	frame #24	1 sec	16 frames
		79	Same—more distant		38 sec	frame #10	11 sec	6 frames
		80	Barge pushing off from shore		49 sec	frame #16	5 sec	24 frames
		81	Poling barge upstream		55 sec	frame #10	4 sec	15 frames
FIG. 36	p.48	82	Distant shot of barge being rowed up river		59 sec	frame #25	4 sec	10 frames
FIG. 37	p.48	83	Sky and vultures	19 min	4 sec	frame #5	3 sec	22 frames
FIG. 38	p.48	84	Corpse floats in river		7 sec	frame #27	4 sec	27 frames
FIG. 39	p.49	85	Mithai Lal worships in his house		12 sec	frame #24	41 sec	8 frames
		86	Paraffin candle		54 sec	frame #2	3 sec	0 frames
FIG. 40	p.50	87	Mithai Lal blows conch shell		57 sec	frame #2	54 sec	13 frames
		88	Close-up of deity with marigolds	20 min	51 sec	frame #15	3 sec	15 frames
FIG. 41	p.51	89	Mithai Lal bangs head on floor		55 sec	frame #0	31 sec	26 frames

FIG #	PAGE #	SHOT #	DESCRIPTION	SHOT BEGINS			SHOT LENGTH	
		90	Puppy dog at marigold stringing	0 hr 21 min	26 sec	frame #26	7 sec	16 frames
		91	Distant shot—same		34 sec	frame #12	3 sec	3 frames
		92	Woman's face in profile		37 sec	frame #15	2 sec	25 frames
FIG. 43	p. 53	93	Puppy gnaws marigold blossom		40 sec	frame #10	13 sec	15 frames
FIG. 42	p. 53	94	Infant asleep foreground—marigold stringing background		53 sec	frame #25	3 sec	6 frames
		95	Close shot—puppy sleeps, woman threads marigolds		57 sec	frame #1	4 sec	13 frames
		96	Handprints and marigolds	22 min	1 sec	frame #14	2 sec	26 frames
		97	Traveling shot up river—calisthenics on ghats		4 sec	frame #10	5 sec	7 frames
FIG. 44	p. 54	98	Traveling shot of man squatting on ghat		9 sec	frame #17	2 sec	2 frames
		99	Traveling shot on river, past sandboat sterns		11 sec	frame #19	23 sec	26 frames
		100	Sand workers carry sand ashore		35 sec	frame #15	10 sec	16 frames
		101	Drowned dog foreground—sandboats in distance		46 sec	frame #1	3 sec	0 frames
		102	Marigold bundle on bicycle		49 sec	frame #1	4 sec	4 frames
		103	Marigolds on rickshaw		53 sec	frame #5	3 sec	25 frames
		104	Marigolds carried on head through traffic		57 sec	frame #0	4 sec	6 frames
		105	Marigolds on rickshaw through traffic	23 min	1 sec	frame #6	4 sec	13 frames
FIG. 45	p. 54	106	Cow eats marigolds		5 sec	frame #19	3 sec	27 frames
FIG. 46	p. 54	107	Procession in Manikarnika gully. Cow runs at camera		9 sec	frame #16	8 sec	6 frames
		108	Closer procession		17 sec	frame #22	10 sec	29 frames
FIG. 47	p. 55	109	Woman prays at Ragul Pandit's shrine		28 sec	frame #21	30 sec	9 frames
		110	Ragul worshiping with water.		59 sec	frame #0	10 sec	20 frames
		111	Different angle—same	24 min	9 sec	frame #20	7 sec	21 frames
		112	Different angle—same		17 sec	frame #11	4 sec	15 frames
		113	Different angle—same—exterior in background		21 sec	frame #26	8 sec	19 frames
FIG. 48	p. 55	114	Woman gyrates on balcony		30 sec	frame #15	21 sec	19 frames
		115	Bamboo worker		52 sec	frame #4	8 sec	7 frames
FIG. 49	p. 56	116	Closer—same	25 min	0 sec	frame #11	13 sec	0 frames
		117	Different angle—same		13 sec	frame #11	6 sec	14 frames
		118	Different angle—constructing ladder		19 sec	frame #25	5 sec	17 frames
		119	Different angle—same		25 sec	frame #12	8 sec	0 frames
		120	Different angle—same		33 sec	frame #12	5 sec	27 frames

FIG #	PAGE #	SHOT #	DESCRIPTION	SHOT BEGINS			SHOT LENGTH	
		121	Man ties ladder	0 hr 25 min	39 sec	frame #9	21 sec	17 frames
		122	Different angle—works on ladder	26 min	0 sec	frame #26	3 sec	4 frames
		123	Different angle—ties other end		4 sec	frame #0	35 sec	21 frames
		124	Props ladder against wall		39 sec	frame #21	15 sec	5 frames
FIG. 50	p.57	125	Laddermaker smokes		54 sec	frame #26	10 sec	3 frames
FIG. 51	p.57	126	Man sleeping on bamboo poles—street beyond	27 min	4 sec	frame #29	3 sec	7 frames
FIG. 52	p.59	127	Outside Mukhti Bhavan—dog and cow		8 sec	frame #6	14 sec	4 frames
FIG. 53,54	p.59	128	Washing courtyard at Mukhti Bhavan—tilt to ceiling		22 sec	frame #10	33 sec	1 frames
		129	Start of visit to dying women		55 sec	frame #11	20 sec	9 frames
FIG. 55	p.61	130	Attendants go up the stairs	28 min	15 sec	frame #20	14 sec	24 frames
		131	In dying woman's room		30 sec	frame #14	13 sec	18 frames
		132	Waving flame		44 sec	frame #2	6 sec	10 frames
FIG. 56	p.62	133	Flame and woman gesturing		50 sec	frame #12	9 sec	18 frames
FIG. 57	p.62	134	Different angle—same	29 min	0 sec	frame #0	4 sec	21 frames
		135	Giving Ganges water		4 sec	frame #21	57 sec	10 frames
FIG. 58	p.63	136	Another dying woman	30 min	2 sec	frame #1	39 sec	16 frames
FIG. 59	p.64	137	Attendants descend stairs		41 sec	frame #17	15 sec	2 frames
FIG. 60	p.64	138	They cross courtyard—seen from balcony		56 sec	frame #19	17 sec	7 frames
FIG. 61	p.64	139	Dog gnaws carcass on far shore	31 min	13 sec	frame #26	11 sec	15 frames
FIG. 62	p.65	140	Same—city in background		25 sec	frame #11	5 sec	8 frames
		141	Sand workers load sand—far shore		30 sec	frame #19	11 sec	3 frames
FIG. 63	p.66	142	Sand barge on Ganges goes up river		41 sec	frame #22	7 sec	14 frames
FIG. 64	p.67	143	Corpse on a boat going to cremation ground		49 sec	frame #6	9 sec	18 frames
FIG. 65	p.68	144	Blind man descends stairway		58 sec	frame #24	25 sec	20 frames
		145	Reverse—same—continues down to river	32 min	24 sec	frame #14	10 sec	28 frames
FIG. 66	p.68	146	Dead donkey dragged down steps to river		35 sec	frame #12	7 sec	18 frames
		147	Same—reverse angle		43 sec	frame #0	5 sec	7 frames
		148	Same—different angle		48 sec	frame #7	9 sec	4 frames
		149	Dead dog dragged down steps		57 sec	frame #11	9 sec	6 frames
FIG. 67	p.68	150	Sweepers clean steps	33 min	6 sec	frame #17	13 sec	20 frames
FIG. 68	p.70	151	Cow devours marigolds		20 sec	frame #7	16 sec	29 frames

FIG #	PAGE #	SHOT #	DESCRIPTION	SHOT BEGINS			SHOT LENGTH	
FIG. 69	p.70	152	Shopkeeper sells kites	0 hr 33 min	37 sec	frame #6	4 sec	3 frames
		153	Gully—people walking		41 sec	frame #9	4 sec	17 frames
		154	Hungry dogs lap spilled milk		45 sec	frame #26	3 sec	0 frames
		155	Vultures circle Dom Raja's house		48 sec	frame #26	7 sec	0 frames
		156	Procession down Manikarnika gully—distant shot		55 sec	frame #26	7 sec	21 frames
		157	Woman buys marigolds—bull passes	34 min	3 sec	frame #17	14 sec	2 frames
FIG. 70	p.71	158	Singing beggar in Manikarnika Ghat		17 sec	frame #19	37 sec	11 frames
FIG. 71	p.72	159	Dog shits on steps		55 sec	frame #0	6 sec	24 frames
		160	Dom sweeps wood-weighing courtyard	35 min	1 sec	frame #24	3 sec	27 frames
		161	Doms split log		5 sec	frame #21	5 sec	10 frames
		162	Child plays with wood scale		11 sec	frame #1	3 sec	0 frames
FIG. 72	p.73	163	Doms splitting wood		14 sec	frame #1	7 sec	10 frames
		164	Corpse on way to ghat—dog foreground		21 sec	frame #11	3 sec	18 frames
		165	Corpse carried down stairway		24 sec	frame #29	8 sec	0 frames
FIG. 73	p.73	166	Doms weigh wood		32 sec	frame #29	7 sec	13 frames
FIG. 74	p.74	167	Same—different angle		40 sec	frame #12	15 sec	23 frames
FIG. 75	p.74	168	Corpse carried down gully	35 min	56 sec	frame #5	2 sec	24 frames
		169	Piling wood after weighing		58 sec	frame #29	3 sec	10 frames
		170	Loading wood onto a man	36 min	2 sec	frame #9	5 sec	20 frames
		171	Same—different angle		7 sec	frame #29	7 sec	8 frames
		172	Wood-carrier descends stairs		15 sec	frame #7	6 sec	15 frames
FIG. 76	p.75	173	Empty scale swings		21 sec	frame #22	5 sec	17 frames
FIG. 77	p.75	174	Wood barge rowed up river		27 sec	frame #9	16 sec	17 frames
		175	Traveling shot past washer people		43 sec	frame #26	19 sec	0 frames
		176	From wood barge—rower in foreground	37 min	2 sec	frame #26	12 sec	28 frames
		177	Rower—city in background		15 sec	frame #24	6 sec	7 frames
		178	Dom Raja's house—vultures circle		22 sec	frame #1	6 sec	9 frames
		179	Tiger and vultures from balcony		28 sec	frame #10	2 sec	14 frames
FIG. 78	p.75	180	Woman sweeps courtyard		30 sec	frame #24	7 sec	6 frames
FIG. 80	p.76	181	Dom Raja and attendants		38 sec	frame #0	50 sec	1 frames
FIG. 79	p.76	182	Dom Raja rises and leaves house	38 min	28 sec	frame #1	22 sec	14 frames

FIG #	PAGE #	SHOT #	DESCRIPTION	SHOT BEGINS	SHOT LENGTH
		183	Dom Raja starts into city	0 hr 38 min 50 sec frame #15	7 sec 24 frames
FIG. 81	p. 77	184	Water buffalo descends stairway	58 sec frame #9	5 sec 5 frames
		185	Washing Mukhti Bhavan courtyard	39 min 3 sec frame #14	11 sec 22 frames
		186	Attendants sing in anteroom	15 sec frame #6	13 sec 9 frames
FIG. 82	p. 77	187	Man arrives with ladder	28 sec frame #15	11 sec 6 frames
FIG. 83	p. 77	188	Ladder leans against building	39 sec frame #21	1 sec 20 frames
FIG. 84	p. 78	189	Traveling shot down stairway	41 sec frame #11	15 sec 9 frames
FIG. 85	p. 78	190	Reverse shot of corpse being carried downstairs	56 sec frame #20	19 sec 14 frames
		191	Corpse laid on courtyard	40 min 16 sec frame #4	14 sec 15 frames
		192	Ladder put down by corpse	30 sec frame #19	9 sec 2 frames
		193	Corpse lifted to ladder	39 sec frame #21	13 sec 8 frames
FIG. 86	p. 78	194	Men tie corpse to ladder	52 sec frame #29	17 sec 5 frames
		195	Same—closer	41 min 10 sec frame #4	14 sec 0 frames
		196	Silk draped on corpse	24 sec frame #4	3 sec 20 frames
		197	Readying marigolds for corpse	27 sec frame #24	23 sec 12 frames
FIG. 87	p. 79	198	Tying marigolds onto corpse	51 sec frame #6	7 sec 10 frames
		199	Men singing	58 sec frame #16	4 sec 1 frames
		200	Relatives circle corpse	42 min 2 sec frame #17	31 sec 9 frames
		201	Woman in shadows under arch	33 sec frame #26	2 sec 26 frames
		202	Relatives lift corpse	36 sec frame #22	16 sec 4 frames
		203	Corpse carried out of Mukhti Bhavan	52 sec frame #26	11 sec 26 frames
		204	Empty courtyard with sparrows	43 min 4 sec frame #22	3 sec 7 frames
		205	Corpse being carried out into street	7 sec frame #29	8 sec 18 frames
FIG. 88	p. 80	206	Washing courtyard in Mukhti Bhavan	16 sec frame #17	22 sec 15 frames
FIG. 89	p. 80	207	Oar in water—wood boat	39 sec frame #2	9 sec 27 frames
		208	Back of wood boat and oarsman—city in background	48 sec frame #29	6 sec 11 frames
		209	Different angle—oarsman	55 sec frame #10	11 sec 5 frames
		210	Procession in Manikarnika gully	44 min 6 sec frame #15	10 sec 20 frames
		211	Child and calf watch	17 sec frame #5	2 sec 12 frames
FIG. 90	p. 81	212	Dog scratches fleas at Manikarnika	19 sec frame #17	7 sec 4 frames
FIG. 91	p. 81	213	Sand barge from the bow	26 sec frame #21	10 sec 18 frames

FIG #	PAGE #	SHOT #	DESCRIPTION	SHOT BEGINS				SHOT LENGTH	
		214	Man poles sand barge	0 hr 44 min	37 sec	frame #9		9 sec	25 frames
		215	Different angle—same		47 sec	frame #4		13 sec	16 frames
FIG. 92	p.81	216	Feet of man poling barge	45 min	0 sec	frame #20		6 sec	5 frames
FIG. 93	p.82	217	Marigolds on bow of barge		6 sec	frame #25		2 sec	14 frames
		218	Cargo of sand—man poling in background		9 sec	frame #9		10 sec	5 frames
		219	Sand spills into river over gunwhale		19 sec	frame #14		2 sec	22 frames
		220	Boat carrying child's corpse—body dumped in river		22 sec	frame #6		23 sec	10 frames
		221	Oar in water—wood barge		45 sec	frame #16		8 sec	23 frames
		222	Oarsman in wood boat—head and shoulders		54 sec	frame #9		13 sec	2 frames
		223	Steaming cremation platform	46 min	7 sec	frame #11		2 sec	3 frames
FIG. 94	p.82	224	Empty scale		9 sec	frame #14		6 sec	16 frames
		225	Wood barge landing—Manikarnika		16 sec	frame #0		14 sec	9 frames
		226	Oarsman stows oar		30 sec	frame #9		12 sec	25 frames
		227	Oarsman stows other oar, ties up wood barge		43 sec	frame #4		28 sec	23 frames
		228	Water buffalo at river's edge—Manikarnika	47 min	11 sec	frame #27		20 sec	23 frames
FIG. 95	p.83	229	Wood scale foreground		32 sec	frame #20		4 sec	17 frames
		230	Lingam in shrine with birds		37 sec	frame #7		3 sec	22 frames
FIG. 96	p.83	231	Closer—same		40 sec	frame #29		6 sec	8 frames
FIG. 97	p.84	232	Women pick over embers		47 sec	frame #7		7 sec	7 frames
		233	Man drops load of wood		54 sec	frame #14		8 sec	28 frames
		234	Water buffalo looks out over parapet		3 sec	frame #12		3 sec	19 frames
		235	Weighing out wood	48 min	7 sec	frame #1		11 sec	13 frames
		236	Woman picks over embers		18 sec	frame #14		10 sec	8 frames
FIG. 98	p.84	237	Man drops load of wood		28 sec	frame #22		17 sec	17 frames
		238	Dog sniffs embers		46 sec	frame #9		10 sec	16 frames
		239	Man prepares to launch repaired boat		56 sec	frame #25		12 sec	0 frames
FIG. 99	p.86	240	Carpenter displays tools		8 sec	frame #25		6 sec	25 frames
		241	Marigolds	49 min	15 sec	frame #20		2 sec	1 frames
		242	Carpenter's assistant makes yellow handprints		17 sec	frame #21		14 sec	19 frames
FIG. 100	p.87	243	Same—different angle		32 sec	frame #10		10 sec	10 frames
		244	Same—port side		42 sec	frame #20		4 sec	4 frames

FIG #	PAGE #	SHOT #	DESCRIPTION	SHOT BEGINS	SHOT LENGTH
		245	Same—different angle	0 hr 49 min 46 sec frame #24	11 sec 2 frames
FIG. 101	p.87	246	Procession at Manikarnika	57 sec frame #26	7 sec 29 frames
		247	Manikarnika background—swing pan to boat	50 min 5 sec frame #25	8 sec 20 frames
		248	Yellow ochre on tools	14 sec frame #15	19 sec 7 frames
FIG. 102	p.88	249	Yellow hands mark the ground	33 sec frame #22	16 sec 25 frames
		250	Marigolds on bow	50 sec frame #17	6 sec 18 frames
		251	Corpse lowered onto pyre	57 sec frame #5	1 sec 25 frames
		252	Carpenter's profile	59 sec frame #0	2 sec 27 frames
		253	Carpenter ties strings	51 min 1 sec frame #27	6 sec 10 frames
		254	Carpenter makes offering	8 sec frame #7	2 sec 4 frames
		255	Carpenter circles boat clockwise, offering water	10 sec frame #11	24 sec 25 frames
		256	Carpenter hammers hull, walking clockwise	35 sec frame #6	3 sec 23 frames
		257	Continuation—same shot	38 sec frame #29	10 sec 12 frames
		258	Men swing boat around	49 sec frame #11	10 sec 0 frames
FIG. 103	p.89	259	Blessing boat with river water	59 sec frame #11	6 sec 20 frames
FIG. 104	p.89	260	Pouring water on face of corpse	52 min 6 sec frame #1	4 sec 19 frames
		261	Launching boat	10 sec frame #20	23 sec 0 frames
		262	Procession—Manikarnika	33 sec frame #20	14 sec 10 frames
		263	Rowing "newborn" boat	48 sec frame #0	6 sec 6 frames
		264	Immersing corpse—Manikarnika	54 sec frame #6	9 sec 18 frames
		265	Newborn boat rowed into river	53 min 3 sec frame #24	5 sec 13 frames
		266	Carpenter with marigolds	9 sec frame #7	10 sec 12 frames
		267	Marigold wreath on bow of boat traveling in river	19 sec frame #19	5 sec 1 frames
FIG. 105	p.89	268	Oar in water	24 sec frame #20	8 sec 1 frames
		269	Corpse on roof of motorcycle taxi	32 sec frame #21	9 sec 11 frames
		270	Corpse carried through streets	42 sec frame #2	4 sec 27 frames
		271	Man on bicycle with marigolds	46 sec frame #29	4 sec 16 frames
		272	Laborer pushing load	51 sec frame #15	3 sec 11 frames
		273	Same—different angle	54 sec frame #26	6 sec 16 frames
		274	Men carry corpse	54 min 1 sec frame #12	6 sec 29 frames
		275	Same—different angle	8 sec frame #11	7 sec 24 frames

FIG #	PAGE #	SHOT #	DESCRIPTION	SHOT BEGINS		SHOT LENGTH	
				0 hr 54 min			
		276	Marigolds carried on head	16 sec	frame #5	2 sec	29 frames
		277	Marigold bundle through traffic	19 sec	frame #4	3 sec	22 frames
		278	Laborer pushes load	22 sec	frame #26	8 sec	29 frames
		279	Corpse carried	31 sec	frame #25	2 sec	9 frames
FIGS. 106, 107	p. 90	280	Same—different angle into gulley	34 sec	frame #4	17 sec	21 frames
		281	Blind man, traveling shot from behind	51 sec	frame #25	29 sec	7 frames
FIG. 108	p. 91	282	Dog cowers	55 min 21 sec	frame #2	4 sec	5 frames
		283	Marigold sellers—procession passes	25 sec	frame #7	12 sec	19 frames
		284	Woman watches from doorway	37 sec	frame #26	1 sec	20 frames
		285	Procession in gulley right to left—2 corpses	39 sec	frame #16	28 sec	6 frames
		286	Traveling shot up stairway	56 min 7 sec	frame #22	3 sec	18 frames
FIG. 109	p. 91	287	Man urinates	11 sec	frame #10	2 sec	17 frames
FIG. 110	p. 91	288	Child splits wood	13 sec	frame #27	5 sec	17 frames
		289	Closer—same	19 sec	frame #14	6 sec	8 frames
FIG. 111	p. 92	290	Dead puppy	25 sec	frame #22	1 sec	28 frames
		291	Dom Raja buttons shirt	27 sec	frame #20	14 sec	21 frames
		292	Corpse goes down stairs	42 sec	frame #11	3 sec	11 frames
FIG. 112	p. 92	293	Dom Raja puts on cap	45 sec	frame #22	13 sec	14 frames
FIG. 113	p. 92	294	Spinning thread	59 sec	frame #6	2 sec	29 frames
		295	Pan up to man on roof spinning	57 min 2 sec	frame #5	5 sec	29 frames
		296	Arranging wood pile	8 sec	frame #4	6 sec	8 frames
		297	Man drops load of wood	14 sec	frame #12	9 sec	8 frames
		298	Dom Raja watches	23 sec	frame #20	4 sec	4 frames
FIG. 114	p. 93	299	Sparrow at Dom Raja's knee	27 sec	frame #24	6 sec	28 frames
		300	Dom Raja speaks	34 sec	frame #22	11 sec	24 frames
FIG. 115	p. 94	301	Dom sweeps handrail	46 sec	frame #16	13 sec	19 frames
FIG. 116	p. 94	302	Water buffalo watches	58 min 0 sec	frame #5	11 sec	4 frames
FIG. 117	p. 94	303	Man weeps	11 sec	frame #9	17 sec	28 frames
		304	Carrying wood from barge	29 sec	frame #7	7 sec	12 frames
		305	Woodcarrier near edge of river	36 sec	frame #19	15 sec	26 frames
		306	Man drops load of wood	52 sec	frame #15	4 sec	24 frames

MAKING **FOREST OF BLISS**

FIG #	PAGE #	SHOT #	DESCRIPTION	SHOT BEGINS				SHOT LENGTH	
FIG. 118	p.97	307	Woodcarrier goes upstairs — puppy tries to follow	0 hr	58 min	57 sec	frame #9	26 sec	27 frames
FIG. 119	p.97	308	Corpse goes past Dom Raja down stairs		59 min	24 sec	frame #6	26 sec	20 frames
		309	Puppy staggers up stairs			50 sec	frame #26	12 sec	23 frames
FIG. 120	p.98	310	Dom Raja argues with mourners	1 hr	0 min	3 sec	frame #19	54 sec	0 frames
FIG. 121	p.101	311	Man paints wall			57 sec	frame #19	6 sec	11 frames
		312	Puppy still staggering		1 min	4 sec	frame #0	9 sec	21 frames
FIG. 122	p.101	313	Corpse carried past charcoal gleaners			13 sec	frame #21	8 sec	14 frames
		314	Dom Raja talks and drinks			22 sec	frame #5	19 sec	26 frames
		315	Servant brings food to Dom Raja			42 sec	frame #1	5 sec	15 frames
		316	Dom Raja eats			47 sec	frame #16	17 sec	11 frames
FIG. 123	p.102	317	Closer — same		2 min	4 sec	frame #27	41 sec	24 frames
		318	Mithai Lal at home healing a patient			46 sec	frame #21	26 sec	0 frames
FIG. 124	p.102	319	Mithai Lal holds flame		3 min	12 sec	frame #21	28 sec	4 frames
		320	Man worships at Mithal Lal's shrine			40 sec	frame #25	43 sec	14 frames
FIG. 125	p.102	321	Mithai Lal begins to cure patient		4 min	24 sec	frame #9	56 sec	13 frames
FIG. 126	p.104	322	Different angle — same		5 min	20 sec	frame #22	9 sec	23 frames
		323	Face of girl			30 sec	frame #15	2 sec	26 frames
		324	Man drops load of wood at Manikarnika			33 sec	frame #11	5 sec	15 frames
		325	Corpses at Manikarnika waiting			38 sec	frame #26	23 sec	28 frames
FIG. 127	p.104	326	Immersing corpse in Ganges		6 min	2 sec	frame #24	31 sec	16 frames
FIG. 128	p.104	327	Dogs near corpses			34 sec	frame #10	8 sec	5 frames
FIG. 129	p.105	328	Dom providing sacred fire			42 sec	frame #15	10 sec	24 frames
		329	Corpse carried down steps past Dom Raja			53 sec	frame #9	11 sec	6 frames
		330	Mourner carrying fire past reclining water buffalo		7 min	4 sec	frame #15	11 sec	15 frames
		331	Building a pyre			16 sec	frame #0	4 sec	22 frames
		332	Closer — same			20 sec	frame #22	3 sec	9 frames
		333	A dog and young man scavenge in a dead fire			24 sec	frame #1	8 sec	15 frames
FIG. 130	p.105	334	Chief mourner lights funeral pyre beyond boat			32 sec	frame #16	30 sec	4 frames
		335	Dog at water's edge		8 min	2 sec	frame #20	3 sec	26 frames
		336	Child drinks from broken pipe			6 sec	frame #16	7 sec	25 frames
FIG. 131	p.106	337	Body burning			14 sec	frame #11	13 sec	14 frames

FIG #	PAGE #	SHOT #	DESCRIPTION	SHOT BEGINS				SHOT LENGTH	
		338	Doms scavenge clothing	1 hr 8 min	27 sec	frame #25		26 sec	9 frames
		339	Dom Raja being paid		54 sec	frame #4		26 sec	20 frames
FIG. 132	p.107	340	Dom kicks refuse off porch	9 min	20 sec	frame #24		14 sec	28 frames
		341	Two bracelets near Dom Raja		35 sec	frame #22		2 sec	25 frames
		342	Women mourn above burning ground		38 sec	frame #17		9 sec	9 frames
		343	Dom Raja injected		47 sec	frame #26		22 sec	4 frames
FIG. 133	p.108	344	Sparrows peck at seeds—river in background	10 min	10 sec	frame #0		4 sec	29 frames
		345	Mourner heaves skull into river		14 sec	frame #29		3 sec	2 frames
		346	Dhoti drying over funeral embers		18 sec	frame #1		3 sec	25 frames
FIG. 134	p.108	347	Chief mourner breaks pot on pyre		21 sec	frame #26		3 sec	9 frames
FIG. 135	p.108	348	Dom splits skull of corpse with bamboo pole		25 sec	frame #5		4 sec	4 frames
		349	Relatives dismember litter		29 sec	frame #9		2 sec	25 frames
		350	Water buffalo and sobbing man		32 sec	frame #4		4 sec	5 frames
		351	Dom carrying pile of wood		36 sec	frame #9		1 sec	20 frames
		352	Dom drops tongs by sacred fire		37 sec	frame #29		2 sec	7 frames
		353	Two men climb steps past corpse		40 sec	frame #6		2 sec	16 frames
		354	Cow chews abandoned litter		42 sec	frame #22		1 sec	24 frames
		355	Mourner heaves marigolds into the Ganges		44 sec	frame #16		2 sec	13 frames
		356	A torrent of dead embers		46 sec	frame #29		1 sec	23 frames
		357	Wood scale rising		48 sec	frame #22		1 sec	22 frames
		358	Men place corpse on pyre		50 sec	frame #14		2 sec	3 frames
		359	Chief mourner breaks pot		52 sec	frame #17		6 sec	17 frames
		360	Traveling shot—birds perching on bamboo pole in the river		59 sec	frame #4		22 sec	15 frames
FIG. 136	p.109	361	Two dogs menace each other on far shore	11 min	21 sec	frame #19		6 sec	1 frames
FIG. 137	p.109	362	Sail floats past right to left—from far shore		27 sec	frame #20		9 sec	0 frames
		363	Hull of sand barge does the same		36 sec	frame #20		19 sec	4 frames
		364	Same sail passes, more distant—city in background		55 sec	frame #24		10 sec	11 frames
FIG. 138	p.109	365	Young boy flies a kite	12 min	6 sec	frame #5		7 sec	22 frames
		366	Young boy pulls in kite		13 sec	frame #27		5 sec	17 frames
		367	Boat sets out from shore with child's body		19 sec	frame #14		4 sec	25 frames
		368	Young boy intently plays with kite		24 sec	frame #9		5 sec	25 frames

FIG #	PAGE #	SHOT #	DESCRIPTION	SHOT BEGINS	SHOT LENGTH
FIG. 139	p. 110	369	Boat with child's body glides left to right	1 hr 12 min 30 sec frame #4	15 sec 17 frames
		370	Arm of young boy urgently pulling on kite string	45 sec frame #21	6 sec 20 frames
	p. 110	371	Men drop child into river—kite falls behind the boat	52 sec frame #11	20 sec 16 frames
FIG. 140		372	Traveling shot—head and face of sad-eyed buffalo	13 min 12 sec frame #27	6 sec 18 frames
		373	Child pulling in kite	19 sec frame #15	4 sec 15 frames
FIG. 141	p. 111	374	Traveling shot of buffalo's foot up stairway	24 sec frame #0	7 sec 2 frames
		375	Distant shot of sand workers unloading barges	31 sec frame #2	5 sec 4 frames
		376	Different angle—same	36 sec frame #6	4 sec 14 frames
		377	Sand workers pass—low angle	40 sec frame #20	4 sec 14 frames
		378	Sand workers' feet up and down stairway	45 sec frame #4	3 sec 17 frames
		379	Distant shot of ghats and river with sandboats	48 sec frame #21	3 sec 28 frames
		380	Child runs with kite	52 sec frame #19	4 sec 10 frames
		381	Boys play stick and stone game	56 sec frame #29	6 sec 23 frames
		382	Boy running with kite	14 min 3 sec frame #22	8 sec 25 frames
FIG. 142	p. 111	383	Men irrigating marigold field—distant shot	12 sec frame #17	4 sec 24 frames
		384	Closer—arms and bucket	17 sec frame #11	3 sec 25 frames
		385	Man cultivates marigolds	21 sec frame #6	3 sec 3 frames
		386	Traffic in front of Durga temple	24 sec frame #9	9 sec 23 frames
		387	Marigold seller outside Durga temple	34 sec frame #2	8 sec 7 frames
		388	Hands ring temple bell	42 sec frame #9	4 sec 11 frames
		389	Women worshiping—Durga temple	46 sec frame #20	7 sec 11 frames
		390	Same—different angle	54 sec frame #1	8 sec 11 frames
FIG. 143	p. 111	391	Woman ringing temple bell	15 min 2 sec frame #12	2 sec 13 frames
		392	Worshipers, monkeys, and marigolds	4 sec frame #25	4 sec 17 frames
		393	Different angle—same—monkeys steal marigolds	9 sec frame #12	6 sec 29 frames
		394	Worshiper and temple steps	16 sec frame #11	7 sec 10 frames
		395	Worshiper sitting at the Durga temple	23 sec frame #21	6 sec 11 frames
		396	Men praying at Durga temple	30 sec frame #2	3 sec 23 frames
		397	Monkey watching at Durga temple	33 sec frame #25	4 sec 9 frames
		398	Distant shot Durga temple and worshipers	38 sec frame #4	11 sec 26 frames
		399	Interior Durga temple—worshipers	50 sec frame #0	8 sec 17 frames

FIG #	PAGE #	SHOT #	DESCRIPTION	SHOT BEGINS	SHOT LENGTH
		400	Fakir over fire pit at Durga temple	1 hr 15 min 58 sec frame #17	20 sec 8 frames
		401	Girl drawing hopscotch game	16 min 18 sec frame #25	7 sec 10 frames
FIG. 144	p. 112	402	Same—different angle	26 sec frame #5	2 sec 17 frames
		403	Same—continuation—different angle	28 sec frame #22	5 sec 29 frames
		404	Girl tosses stone for hopscotch	34 sec frame #21	4 sec 11 frames
		405	Slow motion hopscotch	39 sec frame #2	9 sec 8 frames
		406	Hopscotch—different angle	48 sec frame #10	6 sec 1 frames
		407	Oar in the water	54 sec frame #11	8 sec 20 frames
		408	Traveling shot past shore—kite in water	17 min 3 sec frame #1	6 sec 11 frames
		409	Young boy reels in kite	9 sec frame #12	7 sec 19 frames
		410	Face and hands of boy reeling in kite	17 sec frame #1	5 sec 20 frames
		411	Sun setting behind city—sky filled with kites	22 sec frame #21	6 sec 26 frames
FIG. 145	p. 113	412	Sun setting behind building—monkey climbs to parapet	29 sec frame #17	32 sec 14 frames
		413	From the river—the fires at Harischandra	18 min 2 sec frame #1	10 sec 26 frames
FIG. 146	p. 114	414	Drummer and arati—Durga temple	12 sec frame #27	16 sec 17 frames
		415	Monkey and temple bells	29 sec frame #14	5 sec 15 frames
		416	Fire from shrine and devotees	34 sec frame #29	9 sec 10 frames
		417	Same—different angle	44 sec frame #9	14 sec 2 frames
		418	Mithai Lal begins temple seance	58 sec frame #11	54 sec 10 frames
		419	Different angle—Mithai Lal	19 min 52 sec frame #21	28 sec 20 frames
		420	Different angle—Mithai Lal and devotees	20 min 21 sec frame #11	7 sec 13 frames
		421	Mithai Lal above fire pit	28 sec frame #24	32 sec 10 frames
FIG. 147	p. 114	422	Mithai Lal's face chanting over fire	21 min 1 sec frame #4	9 sec 12 frames
		423	Devotee's face and hands	10 sec frame #16	3 sec 20 frames
		424	Mithai Lal's face as he chants—24-frame fade-out	14 sec frame #6	45 sec 15 frames
FIG. 148	p. 115	425	24-frame fade-in to river and boat going left to right	59 sec frame #21	14 sec 10 frames
		426	A dog on the far shore watching	22 min 14 sec frame #1	6 sec 4 frames
		427	Ragul Pandit puts on dhoti	20 sec frame #5	33 sec 22 frames
		428	Ragul worshiping	53 sec frame #27	11 sec 7 frames
		429	Same—prepares chalk for marking his body	23 min 5 sec frame #4	19 sec 26 frames
		430	Ragul worships with candelabra	25 sec frame #0	34 sec 11 frames

FIG #	PAGE #	SHOT #	DESCRIPTION	SHOT BEGINS				SHOT LENGTH	
		431	Same—farther away	1 hr	23 min	59 sec	frame #11	8 sec	1 frames
		432	Same—different angle		24 min	7 sec	frame #12	3 sec	10 frames
FIG. 149	p. 115	433	Same—head and shoulders of Ragul			10 sec	frame #22	5 sec	14 frames
		434	Ragul puts down candelabra			16 sec	frame #6	10 sec	26 frames
		435	Ragul breaks coconut			27 sec	frame #2	6 sec	13 frames
		436	Ragul worhips with coconut and peacock wand			33 sec	frame #15	60 sec	9 frames
		437	Wood-weighing scale		25 min	33 sec	frame #24	1 sec	28 frames
		438	Same—top			35 sec	frame #22	3 sec	3 frames
		439	Ragul chanting			38 sec	frame #25	9 sec	26 frames
		440	Dogs prowl the burning ground—seen from far shore			48 sec	frame #21	3 sec	24 frames
		441	Traveling shot of worshipers in shrine			52 sec	frame #15	10 sec	0 frames
		442	Dog contemplates corpse in river		26 min	2 sec	frame #15	6 sec	22 frames
		443	Ragul worshiping			9 sec	frame #7	10 sec	2 frames
		444	Wood barge rowed right to left—seen from far shore			19 sec	frame #9	3 sec	5 frames
		445	Ragul offers holy food			22 sec	frame #14	16 sec	3 frames
FIG. 150	p. 116	446	Men dismantle ladder at Manikarnika			38 sec	frame #17	3 sec	7 frames
	p. 116	447	Ragul offers holy food			41 sec	frame #24	4 sec	8 frames
FIG. 151	p. 116	448	Dog lopes on far shore			46 sec	frame #2	2 sec	0 frames
		449	Ragul offers holy food			48 sec	frame #2	11 sec	15 frames
FIG. 152	p. 116	450	Laden wood barge at Manikarnika Ghat			59 sec	frame #17	4 sec	9 frames
		451	Ragul prays		27 min	3 sec	frame #26	8 sec	21 frames
FIG. 153	p. 117	452	Rowboat disappears in mist—screen left			12 sec	frame #17	63 sec	13 frames
		453	Middle of fade-out/fade-in to end titles		28 min	16 sec	frame #0	31 sec	0 frames
			Start black leader			47 sec	frame #0	6 sec	0 frames
			Last frame			53 sec	frame #0		

Bibliography

Barbash, Ilisa, and Lucien Taylor. *Cross-cultural Filmmaking*:
   *A Handbook for Making Documentary and Ethnographic Films
   and Videos*. Berkeley: University of California Press, 1997.

Barrett, Marvin. "Images of Death." *Parabola* 11, no. 3 (1986). Society
   for the Study of Myth and Tradition.

Braudy, Leo, and Marshall Cohen. *Film Theory and Criticism*: *Introductory
   Readings*. 5th ed. New York: Oxford University Press, 1999.

Crawford, Peter Ian, and David Turton, eds. *Film as Ethnography*.
   Manchester: Manchester University Press, in association with
   the Granada Centre for Visual Anthropology, 1992.
   Distributed by St. Martin's Press.

Eck, Diana L. *Banaras, City of Light*. 1st ed. New York: Knopf, 1982.
   Distributed by Random House.

———   *Darsan: Seeing the Divine Image in India*. 2nd ed. Chambersburg,
   Penn.: Anima Books, 1985.

Fruzzetti, Lina. *The Gift of a Virgin: Women, Marriage, and Ritual
   in a Bengali Society*. 2nd exp. ed. Delhi and New York:
   Oxford University Press, 1993.

Fuller, C. J. *The Camphor Flame: Popular Hinduism and Society in India*.
   Princeton, N. J.: Princeton University Press, 1992.

Kaushik, Meena. "The Symbolic Representation of Death." *Contributions
   to Indian Sociology* 10, no. 2 (1976), pp. 265–92.

Kumar, Nita. *The Artisans of Banaras: Popular Culture and Identity
   1880–1986*. Princeton, N.J.: Princeton University Press, 1988.

Lannoy, Richard. *The Speaking Tree: A Study of Indian Culture
   and Society*. London: Oxford University Press, 1974.

Loizos, Peter. *Innovation in Ethnographic Film: From Innocence
   to Self-consciousness, 1955–1985*. Chicago: University of Chicago
   Press, 1993.

MacDougall, David. *Transcultural Cinema*. Princeton, N.J.: Princeton
    University Press, 1998.

Östör, Ákos. *The Play of the Gods: Locality, Ideology, Structure,
    and Time in the Festivals of a Bengali Town*. Chicago: University
    of Chicago Press, 1980.

———— "Forest of Bliss: Film and Anthroplogy." *East-West Film Journal*
    8, no. 2 (July 1994), pp. 70–104.

Parry, Jonathan. "Ghosts, Greed and Sin: The Occupational Identity
    of Benares Funeral Priests." *Man*, n.s. 15 (1980), pp. 88–111.

———— "Death and Cosmogony in Kashi." *Contributions to Indian
    Sociology*, 15, nos. 1–2 (1981), pp. 337–65.

———— "Sacrificial Death and the Necrophagus Ascetics." In *Death and
    the Regeneration of Life*, edited by Maurice Bloch and Jonathan
    Parry. Cambridge: Cambridge University Press, 1982.

Saraswati, Baidyanath. *Kashi: Myth and Reality of a Classical Cultural
    Tradition*. Simla, India: Institute of Advanced Study, 1975.

———— *The Spectrum of the Sacred: Essays on the Religious
    Traditions of India*. New Delhi: Concept Publishing, 1984.

Sinha, Surajit, and Baidyanath Saraswati. *Ascetics of Kashi:
    An Anthropological Exploration*. Varanasi (Benares): N. K. Bose
    Memorial Foundation, 1978.

Sukul, Kuber Nath. *Varanasi Down the Ages*. Varanasi (Benares):
    Bhargava Bhushan Press, 1974.

———— "The Forest of Bliss Debate." *Society for Visual Anthropology
    Newsletter* 4, nos. 2 and 5 (1988–89). Contributions by
    E. Carpenter, R. Chopra, R. Gardner, A. Moore, Á. Östör,
    G. Reichel-Dolmatoff, J. Ruby, and F. Stahl.

Warren, Charles, ed. *Beyond Document: Essays on Nonfiction Film*.
    Middletown, Conn.: Wesleyan University Press, 1996.
    Contributions by S. Cavell, R. Gardner, P. Lopate, W. Rothman,
    E. Weinberger, et al.